Friedrich Nietzsche

Das griechische Musikdrama
The Greek Music Drama

Selected Other Works by
Friedrich Nietzsche

The Birth of Tragedy

Untimely Meditations

Human, All Too Human

Daybreak

Idylls of Messina

The Gay Science

Thus Spoke Zarathustra

Beyond Good and Evil

On the Genealogy of Morality: A Polemic

The Case of Wagner

Twilight of the Idols

The Antichrist

Nietzsche Contra Wagner

Ecce Homo

Dionysos Dithyrambs

Friedrich Nietzsche

Das griechische Musikdrama
The Greek Music Drama

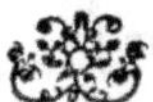

Translated by
PAUL BISHOP

Introduction by
JILL MARSDEN

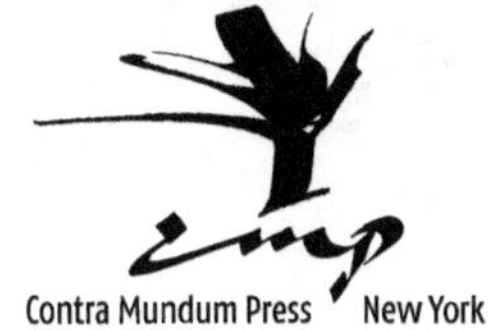

Contra Mundum Press New York

First Contra Mundum Press Edition 2013.
A brief excerpt from this translation was originally published in *The Agonist*, Vol. IV, № 1 (spring 2011).

The German text of this edition of „Das griechische Musikdrama" is excerpted from the *Gesammelte Werke* [Musarion–Ausgabe] ed. Richard Oehler, Max Oehler, and Friedrich Chr. Wurzbach, 33 vols (Munich: Musarion, 1920–1929) vol. 3, *Die Geburt der Tragödie; Aus dem Gedankenkreis der Geburt der Tragödie, 1869–1871*, 169–87.

Library of Congress Cataloguing-in-Publication Data

Nietzsche, Friedrich Wilhelm, 1844–1900

[Das griechische Musikdrama. English.]

The Greek Music Drama / Friedrich Nietzsche;

translated from the original German by Paul Bishop; preface by Paul Bishop; introduction by Jill Marsden

—1st Contra Mundum Press Edition
112 pp., 7 x 10 in.

ISBN 9780983697275

I. Nietzsche, Friedrich.
II. Title.
III. Bishop, Paul.
IV. Translation.
V. Preface.
VI. Marsden, Jill.
VII. Introduction.

2013931780

Table of Contents

Abbreviations: Editions
o

Translator's Preface
ii

Introduction:
In the Depths of Night:
Nietzsche's Tragic Aesthetics in
"The Greek Music Drama"
o

Das griechische Musikdrama
1

The Greek Music Drama
2

Abbreviations: Editions

KSA Friedrich Nietzsche, *Sämtliche Werke: Kritische Studienausgabe*, ed. Giorgio Colli and Mazzino Montinari, 15 vols (Berlin and New York/Munich: Walter de Gruyter/Deutscher Taschenbuch Verlag, 1967–1977 and 1988).

KSB Friedrich Nietzsche, *Sämtliche Briefe: Kritische Studienausgabe*, ed. Giorgio Colli and Mazzino Montinari, 8 vols (Berlin & New York/Munich: Walter de Gruyter/Deutscher Taschenbuch Verlag, 1975–1984).

KGW Friedrich Nietzsche, *Werke: Kritische Gesamtwerkausgabe*, ed. Giorgio Colli and Mazzino Montinari, then Volker Gerhardt, Norbert Miller, Wolfgang Müller-Lauter, Karl Pestalozzi, and the Berlin-Brandenburgische Akademie der Wissenschaften, 40 vols in 9 sections (Berlin and New York: Walter de Gruyter, 1967–2005).

Translator's Preface

In 1870, fresh from his appointment in April 1869 as Extraordinary Professor of classical philology at the University of Basel, Friedrich Nietzsche gave two public lectures in the Basel Museum.[1] The first, delivered on 18 January 1870, was entitled "The Greek Music Drama"; the second, a fortnight later, was entitled "Socrates and Tragedy."[2] Nietzsche's ambition in these lectures was twofold: he was sketching out ideas that were to find definitive expression in *The Birth of Tragedy*, published two years later, and seeking to intervene in the cultural politics of the age by implicitly lending support to Wagner, an unspoken but unmistakable presence in the lectures. In a letter from this period, Nietzsche indicated his awareness that his approach to tragedy was a pluridisciplinary one: "Scholarship, art, & philosophy

1. In a letter to Carl Fuchs, Nietzsche does not sign with his official title, but refers to himself as "formerly Professor of Classical Languages, including Metric," then in his post-script suggests that Fuchs read "a book that few people know — St. Augustine's *De musica* — to see how people in those days understood and enjoyed Horace's meters, how they heard them 'beat time,' where they put the pauses, and so on (*arsis* and *thesis* are mere signs for the beats)." The former "Professor of Classical Languages" concludes his letter by saying "I myself am a 'fugitive and a vagabond on earth.'" KSB 7, S. 176–179; BVN–1886, 688 — Brief an Carl Fuchs von: vermutlich Mitte April 1886: http://www.nietzschesource.org/#eKGWB/BVN-1886,688.
2. For the original text of these two lectures, see KSA 1, 513–549 and KGW III.2, 3–22. This translation is based on "Das griechische Musikdrama," *Gesammelte Werke* [Musarion-Ausgabe] ed. Richard Oehler, Max Oehler, & Friedrich Chr. Wurzbach, 33 vols (Munich: Musarion, 1920-1929) vol. 3, *Die Geburt der Tragödie; Aus dem Gedankenkreis der Geburt der Tragödie, 1869–1871*, 169–87; also in *Werke* [Großoktavausgabe] ed. F. Koegel, 19 vols (Leipzig: Neumann, 1895–1897; 2 edn, 1899–1913) vol. 9, 33–52.

are growing together in me to such an extent," he told his friend, Erwin Rohde, "that if nothing else I shall give birth to centaurs."[3] An earlier part of this letter reflects Nietzsche's passionate commitment to ancient Greece and his almost existential sense of loyalty to Greek culture — as well as his elevated notion of academic life:

> Every day I get to like the Hellenic world more and more. There is no better way of approaching close to it than that of indefatigably cultivating one's own little self. The degree of culture I have attained consists in a most mortifying admission of my own ignorance. The life of a philologist striving in every direction of criticism and yet a thousand miles away from Greek antiquity becomes every day more impossible to me. I even doubt if I shall ever succeed in becoming a proper philologist. If I cannot succeed incidentally, as it were, I shall never succeed.[4]

Arguably the most important aspect of Nietzsche's first lecture on the Greek music drama is his insistence on the relevance for modernity of the ancient conception of tragedy; or rather on the possibility of its relevance being rediscovered. For his lecture is, as Silk and Stern noted, "a public lament over the inability of citizens of the modern world to respond to life as 'whole beings,' above all in the sphere of art,"[5] and behind the argument about the *Gesamtkunstwerk* or "total work of art" lies a plea for a richer, fuller mode of life, one in which — in contrast to the Cartesian tradition, and to the denigration of the body in Western philosophy in general — we undertake to recuperate the total economy of the body and become more holistic beings. And let us hear the latter term not in any mawkish contemporary spiritual sense, but in strictly Nietzschean terms of *Ganzheit*.[6]

3. Nietzsche to Erwin Rohde of late January and 15 February 1870 (KSB 3, 95).
4. KSB 3, 94; *Selected Letters of Friedrich Nietzsche*, ed. Oscar Levy, tr. Anthony M. Ludovici (London and New York: Heinemann, 1921) 62–63.
5. M.S. Silk & J.P. Stern, *Nietzsche on Tragedy* (Cambridge: Cambridge University Press, 1981) 191.
6. Cf. this characteristic passage on Nietzsche's conception of *Ganzheit*: ☞

During a visit to Tribschen with Rohde, Nietzsche — in a room, it has been suggested, in which a water-color version of Genelli's painting of *Bacchus Among the Muses* was hanging[7] — read out part of his lecture on the music drama. Subsequently, on 19 June 1870, he sent a copy of his two lectures to Cosima Wagner who, on 24 June 1870, responded with the following comments about "The Greek Music Drama":

> How touched I am by the dedication of the two lectures you were kind enough to send me. Accept my warmest thanks for having vouchsafed me this great pleasure. I have now re-read the lecture on the music drama and can only repeat that I regard it as an invaluable vestibule to your Socrates lecture. I could have spared myself the most unnecessary agitation at the time of the first reading had I known by what a warm pulsing description of the Greek art works it had been preceded. Your broad-boughed tree is now rooted in the most glorious past, in the homeland of beauty, and proudly rears its head into the most beautiful dreams of the future. Many details that captivated and stimulated me even during your reading are now indelibly stamped upon my mind. For instance, your comprehension of creation and evolution, of the "*Fanget an!*" ["Just begin!"] in art[8] as well as in nature, and particularly, your views on the high consecration of the drama. Your thoroughly trenchant characterization of the chorus as a separate organism — an idea quite new to me — seems to me to furnish the only correct interpretation of the Greek drama. Moreover,

"Was er wollte, das war Totalität; er bekämpfte das Auseinander von Vernunft, Sinnlichkeit, Gefühl, Wille (— in abschreckendster Scholastik durch Kant gepredigt, den Antipoden Goethe's), er disciplinirte sich zur Ganzheit, er schuf sich…" *Götzen-Dämmerung*, "Streifzüge eines Unzeitgemässen" §49; KSA 6:151–52.

7. See Silk and Stern, *Nietzsche on Tragedy*, 214. For further discussion, see Siegfried Mandel, "Genelli & Wagner: Midwives to Nietzsche's *The Birth of Tragedy*," *Nietzsche-Studien* 19 (1990) 212–229.
8. See *The Mastersingers of Nuremberg*, Act 1, scene 3. Translator's note.

> the bold & striking analogy you draw between the religious dance of the chorus and the *andante*, and between the English tragedy (you mean, of course, the Shakespearean) and the *allegros* of Beethoven, has again demonstrated to me your deeply musical nature, and I think it is not improbable that this striking musical instinct, has given you the key to the innermost secrets of the Greek tragedy, to suffering instead of action — just as if a person had been led through the Indian religion to the philosophy of Schopenhauer.[9]

Two years later, when he published *The Birth of Tragedy*, Nietzsche had added a preface in which he dedicated that work to Wagner, and his *Birth* reprises a number of themes from "The Greek Music Drama."[10]

Looking back at a note written in spring of 1884, Nietzsche claimed, "*I have been the first to discover the tragic*," and that the Greeks, "thanks to their moralistic superficiality," had "misunderstood" it.[11] Yet "The Greek Music Drama" anticipates precisely the later Nietzsche's definition of tragedy when, in *Twilight of the Idols*, he wrote: "The psychology of the orgy as an overflowing feeling of life and energy, within which even pain acts as a stimulus, gave me the key to the concept of the *tragic* feeling."[12] Because it is "affirmation of life even in its strangest and most difficult problems; the will-to-life becoming joyful through the *sacrifice* of its highest types to its own inexhaustibility" that Nietzsche at once qualifies as "Dionysian" and uses as "the bridge to the psychology of the *tragic* poet."[13] In an age when, as Rüdiger Safranski has put it, we live simultaneously in two worlds, one Apollonian, the other Dionysian — exemplified by traveling in the tube or

9. See Cosima Wagner's letter to Nietzsche of 24 June 1870, in Elisabeth Förster-Nietzsche (ed.), *The Nietzsche-Wagner Correspondence*, tr. Caroline V. Kerr (London: Duckworth, 1922) 55–56. Translation modified.
10. For further discussion, see Dennis Sweet, "The Birth of *The Birth of Tragedy*," *Journal of the History of Ideas*, vol. 60, no. 2 (April 1999) 345–359.
11. See KSA 11, 25[95] 33 (cf. *The Will to Power* §1029).
12. *Twilight of the Idols*, "What I Owe to the Ancients" §5; KSA 5, 160.
13. Ibid.

jogging through the park (Apollo) whilst listening to music on an i-pod (Dionysos)[14] — Nietzsche's text, presented as an exercise in philological aesthetics, already speaks to our condition in the way that his great work of cultural history, *The Birth of Tragedy*, expanded and developed.

What follows is a translation of Nietzsche's first lecture, accompanied with interpretative notes aimed at explaining references in his text and providing relevant explanatory material. Inasmuch as this text is, for the first time, being presented in English, it is a 'historic' translation, and as such it seeks to make good the comparative neglect of this lecture in Nietzsche studies — at least in the English-speaking world, where it seems to have been largely neglected. Yet "The Greek Music Drama" leads the reader to the heart of Nietzsche's move from philology to philosophy, anticipating the central themes of *Thus Spoke Zarathustra*.[15]

14. Rüdiger Safranski, *Nietzsche: Biographie seines Denkens* (Munich & Vienna: Hanser, 2000) 97.
15. For their comments on an earlier draft of this translation, I should like to thank Rainer J. Hanshe, Yunus Tuncel, & Friedrich Ulfers, while for advice on musicological aspects of Nietzsche's argument, I am grateful to Martin Dixon and Graham Whitaker.

Introduction

In the Depths of Night: Nietzsche's Tragic Aesthetics in "The Greek Music Drama"

And regarding the origin of the tragic chorus: in those centuries when the Greek body blossomed and the Greek soul foamed over with health, were there perhaps endemic ecstasies?
— Nietzsche, *The Birth of Tragedy*, "Attempt at a Self Criticism" §4; KSA 1, 16[1]

FROM HIS PRESCIENT early writings to the splintered, broken prose of his final days of lucidity, the constant reference point for Nietzsche is the world of the ancient Greeks, the axis about which so much of his philosophy turns. Heir to the classicist conception of the noble simplicity and perfect serenity of Hellenic culture, Nietzsche counter-poses a more volatile, exuberant Greek world, dazzling and inscrutable in equal measure. The public lecture "The Greek Music Drama" (1870), delivered 18th January at the Basel Museum, is the first significant indication of the wholly new approach that Nietzsche would take to the questions of Greek art, music, & tragedy that had so absorbed scholars for centuries. Deceptively austere in tone, its novelty lies in its sustained elaboration of the origin of Greek music drama in the crucible of the *Dionysian*, a focus which also serves to highlight the importance of the chorus, the relationship between poetry and music, and the folk rituals and practices of early Greek culture. Cautioning against the historicizing tendencies of the modern scholar, Nietzsche is as modest in his knowledge claims about the ancients as he is provocative in his speculations. The greatest challenge is made to the philological enterprise as such: "I maintain that Aeschylus and Sophocles are known to us only as textbook-poets, as librettists, which means that we do not know them at all" (6; KSA 1, 517). Indeed, one of Nietzsche's chief aims in the lecture is to question what we can 'know' about the drama of Greek antiquity given that its core element — its music — is lost. In this respect, his approach is already genealogical. Not only does he analyze the desire to emulate the ancient Greeks in modern times, he speculates about the kind of values

1. Translation by Jill Marsden. Hereafter cited as "[JM]."

that their surviving art forms presuppose. Suggesting that the Greek experience of the music drama exceeds the concepts that we might bring to bear on its appraisal, he invites the contemporary thinker to call on quite different intellectual and emotional resources. It will be by means of what he refers to in *Philosophy in the Tragic Age of the Greeks* as the alien and illogical powers — powers of imagination & 'intuition' — that insight into the music drama of antiquity will be achieved.[2] We must begin by learning to think and to feel otherwise.

"The Greek Music Drama" is one of a pair of lectures that Nietzsche delivered in Basel in 1870. Its companion piece, "Socrates & Tragedy," was delivered two weeks after "The Greek Music Drama." Taken together, both lectures are regarded as preparatory pieces for *The Birth of Tragedy*, which Nietzsche published early in 1872. However, whilst much of the substance of the Socrates lecture is integrated into *The Birth of Tragedy*,[3] the relationship of "The Greek Music Drama" to that famous text is much harder to determine. The discussion of the material conditions of Greek theater that dominates "The Greek Music Drama" is scarcely in evidence in *The Birth of Tragedy*, whilst the diatribe against scholars that appears to motivate this account likewise barely features in the later work. Most striking of all is the absence of the Apollonian from any consideration of the origin of Greek art in Nietzsche's January 1870 lecture. By mid-1870, just a matter of months later, the Apollonian/Dionysian duality is firmly established in the essay "The Dionysian Worldview," with this dyad already assuming the central features that will be elaborated in *The Birth of Tragedy*.[4]

2. "What then is it that brings philosophical thinking so quickly to its goal? Is it different from the thinking that calculates and measures only by virtue of the greater rapidity with which it transcends all space? No, its feet are propelled by an alien, illogical power — the power of creative imagination." Friedrich Nietzsche, *Philosophy in the Tragic Age of the Greeks*, 40; KSA 1, 814.
3. See §§ 11–14 (KSA 1, 75–96) in particular.
4. The first public mention of the Apollonian/Dionysian distinction is made in the lecture course on *Oedipus Tyrannos* that Nietzsche delivered at the University of Basel during the summer semester of 1870. See John Sallis, *Crossings: Nietzsche and the Space of Tragedy*, 6.

This might seem to indicate that "The Greek Music Drama" is a work of a provisional nature, soon to be surpassed by a more sophisticated formulation of the genesis of tragic theater. However, it is important to resist the temptation to read "The Greek Music Drama" as a mere preface to *The Birth of Tragedy*, as if it has no currency of its own independent of that work. Nietzsche's lecture is important not simply in terms of what it signals for his 'tragic philosophy,' but in terms of what it seeks to secure in its own right.

With this proviso in place, I aim to consider three things. First, I shall address Nietzsche's objections to the 'scholarly' approach to the art of classical antiquity, moving on to consider his striking deployment of a psycho-physiological vocabulary of drives and instincts to account for the dynamic 'Dionysian' potency of the early dramas. Second, I shall reflect on the implications of the fact that "The Greek Music Drama" is Nietzsche's only attempt to account for the genesis of tragedy in purely Dionysian terms. Amid Nietzsche's many tales of the 'origin' of Greek tragedy, this early piece places the greatest weight on the 'natural' order of things. Third, I shall seek to show how through this specific account of the Greek music drama Nietzsche develops an anti-humanist aesthetics of more radical significance than *The Birth of Tragedy* and how, in important ways, this text prefigures his later thinking about the preconditions for any aesthetic activity.

I

In his inaugural lecture as Extraordinary Professor of Classical Philology at the University of Basel, Nietzsche had made the provocative claim that philological activity should be embraced and defined by a philosophical outlook.[5] The beginnings of a very distinctive philosophical outlook are already discernible in "The Greek Music Drama." Nietzsche's argument in outline is that modern art forms are too highly

5. See M. Silk and J.P. Stern, *Nietzsche on Tragedy*, 35.

specialized, stemming from the insights of the scholar rather than from the "life of a people." By contrast, it is claimed that ancient Greek art engages the senses of the "complete human being," conducting him or her to a more profound reality of which the superlative instance is the music drama. With his insistence on appreciating Greek tragedy as a "total art form," Nietzsche's argument pays tacit homage to Wagner's hopes for the "artwork of the future." However, the implications of Nietzsche's lecture reach far beyond such ambitions to embrace more profound philosophical questions about the 'nature' of a genuinely aesthetic culture. In suggesting that drama, even when formalized, retains its roots in something more primal, Nietzsche's "The Greek Music Drama" is much closer in spirit to his later genealogical project of addressing questions of art through the perspective of value for life.[6]

Throughout "The Greek Music Drama," Nietzsche is at pains to stress how dissimilar modern theater is to the dramatic arts of Greece despite seeming to share a common heritage and despite the perhaps inevitable tendency to discern the lineaments of the familiar within the territory of the strange.[7] According to Nietzsche, "a Greek would recognize in our tragedy almost nothing corresponding to his tragedy" (2; KSA 1, 515), although he would be able to recognize how indebted Shakespearean tragedy is in its fundamental structure and character to 'New Comedy' (indeed, the latter was probably the model for the "Romanic-Germanic mystery- & morality-play" that preceded the development of 'theater' as such in Shakespeare's day). Nietzsche asserts that what the Athenians called 'tragedy' is something that today we might call 'Grand Opera,' but there is at best only a faint family resemblance between the two art forms. Unequivocally critical of this "direct mimicry" of the past, he insists that what goes by the name of 'opera' is at best "the distorted image of the music drama of antiquity"

6. See *The Birth of Tragedy*, "Attempt at a Self-Criticism" §2; KSA 1, 14.
7. This contention has to be understood within the context of the highly scholarly but conservative orthodoxy of nineteenth-century philology: the *Altertumswissenschaft* of Friedrich August Wolf.

(2; KSA I, 516). This striving for antique effect at the expense of all other considerations is something which he highlights in further examples: the development in France of "so-called classical tragedy," a drama that has "arisen in a purely scholarly way" (4; KSA I, 516), and the "unbelievable impoverishment of taste" that constitutes "literary music," i.e., music to be read (6; KSA I, 517). If Socratic dialectics came to infect Greek tragedy at the height of its power, its effects are still strikingly virulent in nineteenth-century Europe.

Throughout this litany of complaints, it is evident that Nietzsche makes no essential distinction between the scholars who pass judgment on classical antiquity & the modern artists who ape its external forms:

> The real obstacle to the development of modern art forms is erudition, conscious knowledge, and an excess of knowledge: all growth and development in the realm of art has to take place in the dead of night [*in tiefer Nacht*]. (4; KSA I, 516)

Nietzsche suggests that in the calculated mimicry of the manifest aspects of ancient drama, no consideration is given to the deeper context in which the work was cultivated. Intriguingly, he adds the coda that the modern image of the music drama of antiquity is so 'distorted' because it is developed "without the unconscious force of a natural drive" (4; KSA I, 516). In a similar vein, Nietzsche complains that through the intention of the Florentine scholars of the seventeenth century to revive the "musical effects" of antiquity, "the roots of an unconscious art nourished by the life of the people were cut off or at least severely mutilated" (4; KSA I, 516). These tantalizing assertions are the first signs of a remarkably sustained argument threading through the lecture that will situate the origin of the Greek music drama within a mysterious somatic power, always pulsing below the threshold of consciousness. Whatever fuels this dark creativity in the slumber-less depths of night, it is not mere 'nature' in any pre-critical sense of the term. If art is in some respect a product of 'nature,' it must be remembered that this nature already has its roots in 'life.'

The life of a people is more than their physicality (their 'nature' privatively conceived); it is the reservoir of experiences and practices that constitutes the 'culture' for growth, a transpersonal physiology constantly reinvigorated by its fresh creations. To express it otherwise, the art that "grows out" of life (*ausdem Volksleben herauswachsenden Kunst*) is a modification of life, not something specifically differentiated from it. This nuance is encapsulated in the pregnant phrase "art forces of nature" that Nietzsche will so audaciously call upon in *The Birth of Tragedy* to describe the Apollonian & Dionysian energies that "burst forth" from nature without the mediation of a human artist.[8]

These pulsions and passions are in conflict with the exercise of deliberation. Rejecting the presumption that consciousness, reason, or intentionality is the wellspring of creativity, Nietzsche makes an appeal to the unconscious that bears some resemblance to Schopenhauer's philosophy of pre-representational energetics or 'will.' According to the latter, "unconsciousness is the original & natural condition of all things,"[9] and even when the individual will is "awakened to life out of the night of unconsciousness," unconsciousness still predominates.[10] Like Schopenhauer, the accent in Nietzsche's account is upon the fundamental continuity of human life with nature. To this extent, Nietzsche's thinking about the drives is premised on an unconscious identity of body and 'will,' albeit in a libidinal rather than a metaphysical register.[11]

8. *The Birth of Tragedy* §2; KSA 1, 14.
9. See Arthur Schopenhauer, *The World as Will & Representation*, vol. II, 142.
10. Ibid., 573.
11. It is striking that Nietzsche should adopt Schopenhauer's anti-humanist notion of will, and yet imbue it with materialist rather than metaphysical significance. In fact, in what appears to be a preparatory draft for this section of the lecture in his notebooks, Nietzsche substitutes 'the senses' for the unconscious force of a natural drive, lending further support to the view that his notion of the unconscious should be thought in more physiological than psychological terms: "The opera came into being without any foundation in the senses, in accordance with an abstract theory and the conscious intention to achieve the effects of the ancient drama by these means" (KSA 7, 1[1] 9). It is ☞

To the extent that the body is the locus of unconscious 'natural drives,' it is a pre-personal confluence of impulses, not yet the privatized body of Socratic man. According to Freud, a 'drive' is a "concept on the frontier between the mental and the somatic,"[12] but a drive or instinct can never become the object of consciousness; only the idea representing it can do this. Whilst some profound emotions are felt as bodily stirrings and agitations, there are many desires and affects pressing towards existence that remain unconscious. These unconscious pre-representational impulses do not need to be registered at the level of conceptuality for them to be creative. Again, Freud is instructive on this point, remarking that "repression does not hinder the instinctual representative from continuing to exist in the unconscious," nor "from organizing itself further, putting out derivatives and establishing connections."[13] Freud also suggests that the instinctual representative develops more profusely when withdrawn by repression from conscious influence: "It proliferates in the dark, as it were."[14]

In his appeal to the autonomy of unconscious processes, Nietzsche places enormous emphasis on the non-rational drives. However, we must not assume that simply because the energies of the unconscious are unavailable to representational thought that they are unavailable to 'thought' more generally. For example, Nietzsche suggests that one must call on great feats of imagination and intuition to "discern the original image in this caricature" (6; KSA 1, 517). The task is to present the opera "to our mind's eye in a moment of imaginative power," the hope being that if done in a sufficiently idealized way, "an intuition [*Anschauung*] into the music drama of antiquity" will be granted (6; KSA 1, 517). Bizarre as the recommendation seems, Nietzsche is suggesting that we attempt to transport ourselves through the powers of imagination

---

notable that Nietzsche's Schopenhauerianism in "The Greek Music Drama" should be less orthodox than in *The Birth of Tragedy*, which attempts to graft ontological concepts onto the economy of libidinal drives.

12. Sigmund Freud, "Instincts and Their Vicissitudes," *On Metapsychology*, 118.
13. Sigmund Freud, "Repression," op. cit. 148.
14. Ibid.

to another dimension of thought. If the objectionable 'caricature' of antiquity results from the tendency to perceive the ancients merely as lyric writers, Nietzsche's proposed solution is fundamentally an eliminative one, its success depending on our "excluding from thought in moments of enthusiasm" all distortions. These "moments of enthusiasm" (*begeisterter Stunde*) are more significant than one might suppose because we need to cultivate these exuberant states if we are to connect with the ancient world in the unusual way that Nietzsche recommends. If "we have first of all to learn how one enjoys as a complete human being" (10; KSA 1, 519), it is essential to eschew the habit of taking a work to pieces in order to make it one's own (10; KSA 1, 519). It is worth pointing out that by the time of *The Birth of Tragedy*, Nietzsche is able to assert that we shall have gained much for aesthetic knowledge when we have come to realize the value of supplementing logical insight with the "certainty of intuition [*Anschauung*]" (*The Birth of Tragedy* §1; KSA 1, 25).[15] The term *Anschauung* implies visual perception, something engaging the senses rather than the 'mind' narrowly conceived. One might think of it as a momentary irruption of an unconscious perception into the bright day-lit realm of conscious awareness.

It is through a kind of imaginative leap of this order that Nietzsche encourages his listeners to connect with the ancient Greek world. In a note from this period, he writes that "nothing is more erroneous than to apply our standard of the aestheticizing critical audience to the Greek theater" (KSA 7, 9[9] 274). He claims that, "if one of us were to be suddenly transported back to an Athenian festival performance, he would have the impression of being at an entirely strange & barbaric spectacle" (10; KSA 1, 519). In the bright light of the daytime sun — in "dazzling reality" — one would see an enormous open space overflowing with people, their eyes transfixed on the gaudily masked "superhumanly sized puppets" parading the long, thin stage in their high boots, their bodies padded out with stuffing and supporting "massive headgear" (12; KSA 1, 519–520). Nietzsche details at length the immensely

15. [JM].

demanding feats of vocalization required by these actors, marveling at the "concentration and exercise of human forces" that their protracted preparation demands. This is matched by the exacting limitations within which the dramatic artist was obliged to work. The subject matter of the masterpieces was already well known and there was no imperative to manipulate the plot so as to manufacture suspense or intrigue. Nietzsche then remarks on the solemnity of both actor & spectator in thrall to "an unusual, much-longed-for festive mood" (14; KSA 1, 520), twice contrasting this disposition with the modern theater goer who "in anxious flight" from boredom and self-loathing (14; KSA 1, 520) arrives at the theater with "weary and enervated senses" (18; KSA 1, 522) hoping to find sufficient emotional stimulation to jolt him out of his lassitude.

> In contrast to this audience, which is the straitjacket of our contemporary theater, the Athenian spectator still had the fresh senses of early morning, albeit now in festive mood, when he sat down on the steps of the auditorium. (18; KSA 1, 522)

Senses tingling with anticipation, the happy Athenian drinks the potion of tragedy as if for the first time, savoring the draught for its rareness and its power to perpetually please anew.[16] Nietzsche goes on to make the point that to enjoy drama on rare occasions has the advantage of stimulating senses that have not become accustomed to this specific purpose. In this connection, he cites with approval the view of the architect Gottfried Semper that nothing is more propitious for a work of art than when it is seen "beyond any immediate and vulgar contact with what is close at hand or seen from the usual perspective of human beings" (18; KSA 1, 522). The insight that Nietzsche draws from these reflections is an intriguing one: "it is to the advantage of pictures &

16. Greek mythology and Nietzsche's philosophy abound with instances of recurrence of the 'first time.' This is exemplified in the myth of Demeter, "who rejoices again for the first time when told that she may once more give birth to Dionysus." *The Birth of Tragedy* §10; KSA 1, 72.

plays when they are seen from an unusual angle and perceived differently" (18; KSA 1, 523). In short, the primary aesthetic value of Greek tragedy lay in its ability to transport the spectator beyond his/her everyday awareness into a richer and more expansive state.

We could perhaps go further. For Nietzsche, the poet, actors, chorus, and audience constitute an essential unity, but this unity does not comprise the relation of parts to a whole. By way of illustration he cites with approval Anselm Feuerbach's view about the drama of antiquity as a total work of art. According to Feuerbach, the individual art forms blend together "into an inseparable whole, into a new art form" (8; KSA 1, 518). Newly configured, the ancient drama is like a living organism that cannot be returned to its "components" — unlike the "absolute art forms" of modernity, which fragment life into abstractions: "we are, as it were, torn into little pieces by absolute art forms, and hence enjoy as little pieces, in one moment as ear-men, in another as eye-men, and so on" (8; KSA 1, 518). When Nietzsche emphasizes the need to "enjoy as a complete human being," seemingly the injunction is not to become more fully *human* but to enjoy more *completely*. As we shall see, this is to experience a unity that is both shocking & profound in its allergic resistance to the "single unit."

II

Nietzsche claims that the soul of the Athenian who came to watch tragedy at the great Dionysian festivals still bore "something of that element" from which tragedy had sprung: "the powerful drive of springtime when it bursts forth, a storming and raging in a mixture of emotions" (*der übermächtig hervorbrechende Frühlingstrieb, ein Stürmen und Rasen in gemischter Empfindung*) (14; KSA 1, 521). Tragedy is the fruit of this rising sap, the product of germinal power. It is uncertain here whether Nietzsche's first instinct is libidinal or meteorological, but the anti-humanist tenor is startlingly clear. Tragedy has its origin in the tilt of the earth and the wheeling of the sun into ever-longer days.

The *drive* of springtime is vital, quixotic, intoxicating: a power that draws out the senses beyond their usual thresholds. Most potent when it erupts with sudden fury, the impetus of spring manifests itself in a cocktail of mixed sensibility (*Empfindung*), which Nietzsche assures us is "familiar to all naïve peoples and the whole of nature when spring approaches" (14; KSA 1, 521). Indeed, from the perspective of 'spring,' there is no presumed ownership of emotions: they "burst forth" from nature in a generalized fury, coursing through stems, branches, sexual organs. It is also well known — or so it is claimed — that carnival plays and masquerades were originally such spring festivals that only ceased to flourish owing to the intervention of the Church. We are told that here everything stems from the "deepest instinct" (*tiefster Instinkt*). The monstrous swarming Dionysian throng of ancient Greece had its counterpart in the dancers of St. John & St. Vitus in the Middle Ages, when a crowd growing ever larger in number, sang and danced and leapt from town to town. Provocatively, Nietzsche declares that if the contemporary medical establishment pronounce this phenomenon a "national epidemic of the Middle Ages," it should be remembered that the "ancient drama blossomed forth [*erblüht*] from precisely such a national epidemic" (16; KSA 1, 521). Moreover, he adds that it is to the detriment of the arts today that they "do *not* flow from such an enigmatic source"— as if these bewitching spasms of contagion are inherently superior to artistic 'intentions' of any kind (16; KSA 1, 521).

If modern art suffers from an excess of light, whatever takes place "in deep night" (*in tiefer Nacht*) is seemingly the work of the "deepest instinct" (*tiefster Instinkt*) (4; KSA 1, 521). This recourse to instinct may strike the first-time reader to Nietzsche's lecture as something of an idiosyncrasy; however, it is of particular interest to note that Nietzsche was planning a work entitled "Socrates and Instinct" (KSA 7, 3[73] 79) during 1870, and that the role of instinct is the keynote which unites "The Greek Music Drama" with its companion lecture, "Socrates and Tragedy." In the latter lecture, Nietzsche asserts that

> with all productive natures the unconscious mind straightforwardly produces in a creative and affirmative manner, whereas the conscious mind behaves critically and dissuades. With [Socrates] instinct becomes critic & the conscious mind becomes creator. (KSA 1, 542)

It would be the crudest kind of behaviorism that would commute instincts to mere tics, twitches, and reflexes. As already noted in relation to unconscious drives, the theory of creativity that subtends "The Greek Music Drama" is rooted in the life of a people. Instinctual activity implies a kind of embedded cultural knowledge, a deeply embodied record of a people's values. It is evident from Nietzsche's account that the "deepest instincts" of the Dionysian revelers are positive evaluations of the life of nature. Moreover, Nietzsche's depiction of Greek tragedy, from first to last, is articulated in terms of instincts, "the Dionysian" signifying the religious experience of "the profoundest instinct of life, the instinct for the future of life, for the eternity of life."[17]

This tragic impetus, at once both vital and viral, is an inner modification or transformation of 'nature.' In fact, the operative terms of this essay are fundamentally *energetic*, marking increase and transmission of force, its shoring up and its violent release. The accent falls throughout on the potency of activity rather than the powers of agency. Accordingly, Nietzsche assures us that it is "not from willfulness and deliberate exuberance" that wildly moving crowds "dressed as satyrs & sileni" roam through field and wood (16; KSA 1, 521). On the contrary:

> the all-powerful, so suddenly announced effect of spring here intensifies the powers of life into such an excess that ecstatic conditions, visions, and the belief in one's own enchanted state appear everywhere, and similarly affected individuals stream in hordes across the countryside. (16; KSA 1, 521)

17. *Twilight of the Idols*, "What I Owe to the Ancients" §4; KSA 6, 159.

Excess is the wellspring of the Dionysian, the incontestable intensification of life. Everywhere life thrusts forth and bursts. Buds split, seed cases explode, madness breaks out in peals of frenzied laughter. Intoxicated and entranced, breathing deep, heady draughts of enlivening air, the enraptured throng streams across the landscape in delirial waves, flushing away the torpid human sediment. This flood-tide erodes the boundaries of civilized subjecthood, setting the self adrift. "And here," Nietzsche exclaims, "is the cradle of drama." For drama is not born of a will to disguise oneself or to deceive others. For Nietzsche, drama begins "when a human being steps outside himself and believes himself to be transformed and enchanted" (16; KSA 1, 521).

> In this condition of "being-outside-of-oneself," or ecstasy, only one further step is necessary: we do not return back into ourselves, but turn into another being, so that we ourselves behave like enchanted beings. This is the fundamental reason for our deep astonishment at the sight of the drama: the ground shakes, the belief in the indissolubility and the permanence of the individual. (16; KSA 1, 521–522)

If the humanizing process is commensurate with the repression of sacrificial impulses, the tragic imperative is its contra-flow. It is the socially tamed self that is cast aside, along with the life of the marketplace, the street, the courts of justice. The powers of life are so intensified that the borders of civilized existence cannot *but* be breached. An industrious selfhood dissipates, flows into the dance rhythms of extra-human life. Indeed, when one is outside of oneself and believes oneself to be transformed and enchanted, something magical has *really* happened. When the ground shakes, it sends shock waves through the belief in the indissolubility and the permanence of the individual. The Dionysian reveler who "believes in his transformation" experiences it physiologically. This belief is not abstractly entertained like a hypothesis, a 'might be'; it is deeply felt and physically realized. When "the all-powerful, so suddenly announced effect of spring" kindles the powers of life to a point

of delirial outbreak, a fundamental change ripples through 'nature' as such. These beliefs are real material forces that are registered in beating hearts and pulsing limbs animating the libidinal landscape: "similarly affected individuals stream in hordes across the countryside" (16; KSA 1, 521).

III

Thus far Nietzsche has sought to establish that "something of this Dionysian life of nature could still be found in the soul of the spectators in the heyday [*Blüthezeit*] of the Attic drama" (18; KSA 1, 522). The 'soul' of the spectator is rooted in the rich nutritive element of 'life' that stimulates the "festive mood" and invigorates the senses. Nietzsche's final move in "The Greek Music Drama" is to show how essential this physiological disposition is to the experience of ancient tragedy. This is difficult to appreciate because our understanding of tragedy is compromised by aesthetic expectations based on modern theater. According to Nietzsche, ancient tragedy in its earlier stages concerns itself with "suffering" (*pathos*) rather than "action" (*drama*). Even when dialogue arises and the "plot" is added, "every genuine and serious deed [takes] place off-stage" (28; KSA 1, 527). Because we lack knowledge of how suffering or how "the emotional life as it erupts" (*das Gefühlsleben in seinen Ausbrüchen*) was rendered in a sufficiently moving way, he maintains that we cannot be judicious in our estimation of Aeschylus and Sophocles (32; KSA 1, 528). Since all that remains to us is verse, it can only be guessed at how it was augmented and amplified. The crucial point is that "we lack the competence to deal with a Greek tragedy, because its main effect relies to a large extent on an element that we have lost: on the music" (32; KSA 1, 528).

In making this argument, Nietzsche not only challenges the dominant tendency since Aristotle to conflate the tragic with the dramatic, he also makes the experience of music central to the appreciation of

tragic pathos. Nietzsche claims that the task of converting the suffering of the god and the hero into the strongest possible compassion in the spectators was only partially achieved by the language of the drama. His reasoning is that language serves a primary conceptual function and that it only works on the emotions at an ancillary level, often failing to impact upon them at all. In a Schopenhauerian spirit he asserts that "Music, however, immediately strikes the heart, as the true universal language that is understood everywhere" (32; KSA 1, 528–529). In a note contemporaneous with "The Greek Music Drama," this thought is developed at greater length:

> [Music] contains the universal forms of all the states in which we crave something: it is the symbolism of the drives through and through, and as such is thoroughly comprehensible to everyone in its simplest forms (beat, rhythm).
>
> It is therefore always more universal than any particular plot. It is therefore more comprehensible to us than any given plot: music is therefore the key to the drama. (KSA 7, 1 [49] 23)

When Nietzsche suggests that music is the true universal language which is understood everywhere, he calls upon the "symbolism of the drives" in its "simplest forms" to clarify his proposition. That music is capable of generating sensations of "all the states in which we crave something" is partly due to the rhythmic expectations of progression, development, and resolution set up across the tonal scale. Such patterns are unconsciously incorporated by the listener, whose body pulses with anticipation, straining with tension as dissonant elements attenuate the moment, giving way to a more profound sense of release. Indeed, Nietzsche goes on to argue that what has survived of ancient compositions from antiquity "is reminiscent in its strict rhythmic structure" of the folk song from which it is also suggested that "the entire poetic art and music of antiquity blossomed" (34; KSA 1, 529). In the classical age, the language of words and the language of sounds were not yet separated, and "genuinely Greek

music was inherently vocal music" (34; KSA 1, 529).[18] Nietzsche insists that what poetry & music lacked at the level of harmony, they more than compensated for with their richness at the level of expression. His example in "The Greek Music Drama" is orchestral dancing that was so closely synchronized with the rhythmic periodic structure of the music and the words that "one perceived that music had, in a sense, become visible" (36; KSA 1, 530). In *The Birth of Tragedy*, Nietzsche would argue that "the orgiastic movements of a people immortalize themselves" in the music of the folksong and that stirring Dionysian currents are its substratum and prerequisite.[19] In short, the Greeks expressed the ecstasy of becoming in their tragic art — and it was music that augmented their instincts and their drives.

One thinks back to Nietzsche's scandalous suggestion that the ancient drama 'blossomed' from an epidemic of enchanted singers and dancers. Although he stops short of making the link between the Dionysian state of extreme excitability and the universality of music, it is clear that both of these thoughts are already in place in his 1870

18. According to Babette Babich, ancient Greek poetry and prose lacked accentuation or 'stress,' which meant that the musical rhythmic structure of the ancient Greek verse line was completely determined by language and could not be accentuated and set to music in different ways. The fixed tonic intervals of archaic Greek confined rhythm entirely within the limits of language. In this key sense, ancient Greek music was indistinguishable from speech. This is why Nietzsche is able to assert that ordinary language is the medium of poetry. This also clarifies Nietzsche's point that we need to learn to read with our ears rather than our eyes in order to 'hear' the spirit of the music of the tragic text (just as the ancients were able to visualize their music in the steps of the dance), though he could be signaling toward some synaesthetic form of perception, too. The folk song and lyric poetry are at the core of the music drama, the voice of language as such. If tragedy is born from the folksong, this is because ancient Greek music was primarily vocal. The problem for the modern reader of tragedy is that we are limited to what we can see, being unable to 'hear' with our eyes. Babette E. Babich, "The Science of Words *or* Philology: Music in *The Birth of Tragedy* and the Alchemy of Love in *The Gay Science*," *Rivista di estetica*, n.s., 28 (I/2005) XLV, 59-61.
19. *The Birth of Tragedy* §6; KSA 1, 48.

lecture.[20] Indeed, the experience of ecstasy unsettles the epistemological framework upon which the essential Schopenhauerian opposition between representation (language, words, images) and the "ground of representation" (the non-imagistic will) appears to rely. The empirical relation of a subject of experience to its object is suspended in the ecstatic experience of music, exceeding the epistemological coordinates of the "conscious knowledge" that Nietzsche so maligns. To express it in a more Freudian register, the drives are liberated from object attachment and become free flowing, "un-bound." The Dionysian state names the return of individuated existence to the field of immanence. The affects that are 'felt' are orphaned, dispossessed. Within Dionysian ecstasy, the normative ties and object relations that govern human experience are breached and the drives — the instinctual energies of the body — are registered as intense emotional states. In the music drama, these intense affective states are susceptible to transformation and conversion, rippling through a generalized social body as a line of flight. This vector of migration from individual selfhood is realized in the "unison choral music of the Greeks" (26; KSA 1, 526).

> Although a plurality of persons, musically the chorus does not represent a collective, but an enormous single being endowed with oversized lungs. (26; KSA 1, 525–526)

It is well known that, at its origin, "tragedy was nothing other than a giant choral-song" (24; KSA 1, 524–525). In the proto-dramatic form of Greek tragedy, the 'spectator' as such did not exist. Nietzsche sets out the thought, to be embellished further in *The Birth of Tragedy*, that tragedy was originally a song that was sung from the condition of certain mythological beings — "satyrs and sileni" — who communicated the source of their excitement as votaries of Dionysos. When tragedy becomes formalized as a staged spectacle, the spectators identify with the chorus, who in turn behold the visionary world of the god.

20. See also *Twilight of the Idols*, "Expeditions of an Untimely Man" §10; KSA 6, 117–118.

> First of all, a dithyrambic chorus, composed of men disguised as satyrs and sileni, had to make what had put it into such a state of excitement: it pointed, in a way that was immediately comprehensible to the spectators, to an episode from the story of the struggles and sufferings of Dionysos. (30; KSA 1, 527)

The chorus had to convey what had put it into such a state of agitation. They achieve this through their song, which we might assume stirs the Dionysian life of nature in the souls of the theater goers.[21] The Dionysian dithyramb arouses the ecstatic excitation of the spectators, stimulating their creative identification with the mythological world of the play.

This is as close as Nietzsche gets in "The Greek Music Drama" to drawing the link between the ecstatic dispossession of the Dionysian revelers and the 'universality' of music, but the fact remains that in this unprepossessing early work, Nietzsche is already wholly alert to how fundamental the experience of *ekstasis* is to Greek art. In his later reflections on the "Physiology of Art," Nietzsche would write that "the effect of works of art is to *excite the state which creates art*: ecstasy."[22] Similarly, in *Twilight of the Idols,* Nietzsche would relate the tragic feeling to a surplus of energy,[23] to an orgiastic sensitivity of highly charged nervous systems.

> For art to exist, for any sort of aesthetic activity or perception to exist, a certain physiological precondition is indispensable: intoxication [*Rausch*]. Intoxication must first have heightened the excitability of the entire machine: no art results before that happens.[24]

21. Compare *The Birth of Tragedy* (§8; KSA 1, 63): "Now the dithyrambic chorus was assigned the task of exciting the mood of the listeners to such a Dionysian degree that, when the tragic hero appeared on the stage, they did not see the awkwardly masked human being but rather a visionary figure, born as it were from their own rapture."
22. *The Will to Power* §821; KSA 13, 14[47] 241.
23. *Twilight of the Idols,* "What I Owe to the Ancients" §4; KSA 6, 158.
24. *Twilight of the Idols,* "Expeditions of an Untimely Man" §8; KSA 6, 116.

The ecstatic state of "being-outside-of-self" drives the anti-humanism of Nietzsche's lecture. In many respects, "The Greek Music Drama" has a more anti-humanist tenor than *The Birth of Tragedy* which, in a Schopenhauerian idiom, characterizes the Dionysian as an instance in which the principle of individuation is overcome. By contrast, in "The Greek Music Drama," Nietzsche is much more inclined to speak directly from the perspective of 'nature.' In 1870, tragedy is presented as something that draws the spectator back into a more primordial oneness with nature, a richer and more 'complete' state of awareness. Indeed, "The Greek Music Drama" makes no mention of the Apollonian and there is little hint that this concept will come to play a fundamental role in Nietzsche's thinking about tragedy. In "The Greek Music Drama," Nietzsche is more concerned to give an account of what happens in the "depths of night" than to reflect on what emerges into the light of day as a resplendent vision. With the addition of the Apollonian to Nietzsche's thinking about the birth of tragedy, a space is opened to address the experience of *beauty* so central to the aesthetics of the time. By the same token, the introduction of the Apollonian / Dionysian dyad marks an important shift in Nietzsche's adoption of Schopenhauerian ideas, since the imposition of the appearance/reality distinction signals the end of Nietzsche's thinking of the 'birth' of tragedy as parthenogenetic. It would seem that with the extension of the Schopenhauerian terminology into Nietzsche's thinking about tragedy, the power of the Dionysian is re-situated. Tragedy is born out of a coupling of Apollonian and Dionysian, the emphasis falling upon transgression of the principle of individuation and the experience of ecstasy. It is worth remarking that, under the influence of Schopenhauerian formulations, the two powers are seen as "inherently separate," whereas in Nietzsche's later thinking they are not so obviously opposed. In *Twilight of the Idols* and assorted notes collated in *The Will to Power*, the Apollonian and Dionysian are "both conceived as forms of rapture,"[25] differing in "tempo"[26] rather than in kind.

Nietzsche suggests that those who have grown up "under the influence of the bad habits of modern art" are so inclined to value specialization in art and the separation of art forms that they are no longer able to savor the delights of their combination (34; KSA 1, 529). In his conclusion to "The Greek Music Drama," Nietzsche pays tribute to the synthesis of diverse art forms into an essential unity in the ancient musical drama:

> Tightly bound and yet possessing grace, a diversity and simultaneously a unity, many arts working at their highest level and yet one *single* artwork — that is the ancient music drama. (40; KSA 1, 531)

More fundamentally, perhaps, what Nietzsche had approached in "The Greek Music Drama" was a conception of one *single* nature as immanently self-organizing: "the world as a work of art that gives birth to itself."[27] It is scarcely fortuitous that this lecture should be seeded with the verb *blühen* (to blossom, to bloom), which conveys emergence, growth, and fertility — an irrepressible blossoming power. This is the vibrant culture of the tragic age "when the Greek body blossomed and the Greek soul foamed over with health."[28] The Athenian festival in honor of Dionysos celebrates the rebirth of the god whose dismembered body is scattered like seeds across the earth. The spectator at a tragedy feels this triumph of nature within his own nature as he is drawn into a state of enchantment, realizing in himself

25. Ibid., §10; KSA 6, 117.
26. *The Will to Power* §799; KSA 13, 14[46] 240. For related explorations on the Apollonian and Dionysian and tempo, see: Jill Marsden, "Sensing the Overhuman," *Journal of Nietzsche Studies* 30 (2005) 102–114, & Jill Marsden, *After Nietzsche: Notes Towards a Philosophy of Ecstasy* (Hampshire: Palgrave Macmillan, 2002).
27. Ibid., §796; KSA 12, 2[114] 119.
28. Nietzsche, *The Birth of Tragedy*, "Attempt at a Self Criticism" §4; KSA 1, 16. [JM].

a nascent joy in becoming. At the heart of Greek music drama is intense human communication, the transfer of vibrant life, the brimming over of surplus energies in a rush of exhilaration. These currents of feeling are vectors of attraction: a ripple of excitement at the cool scent of spring, the stirring of anticipation in the rhythmic movements of the dancer, a shiver of pleasure at slipping into the sonorous ocean of the folk song. All around life overcomes itself, bursting into poetry, erupting as dance, blossoming as music.

WORKS CONSULTED

Babette E. Babich, "The Science of Words *or* Philology: Music in *The Birth of Tragedy* & the Alchemy of Love in *The Gay Science*," *Rivista di estetica*, n.s., 28 (I/2005) XLV, 47–78.

Sigmund Freud, *On Metapsychology: The Theory of Psychoanalysis* (Harmondsworth: Pelican, 1984).

Kritische Studienausgabe (KSA), eds Giorgio Colli and Mazzino Montinari (Munich, Berlin, and New York: Walter de Gruyter, 1967–77 and 1988).

Friedrich Nietzsche, *Philosophy in the Tragic Age of the Greeks*, tr. by Marianne Cowan (Chicago: Henry Regnery, 1962).

———, *The Birth of Tragedy*, tr. by Walter Kaufmann (New York: Random House, 1967).

———, *Twilight of the Idols*, tr. by R.J. Hollingdale (Harmondsworth: Penguin, 1968).

———, *Ecce Homo*, tr. by R.J. Hollingdale (Harmondsworth: Penguin, 1979).

———, *The Will to Power*, tr. by R.J. Hollingdale and Walter Kaufmann (New York: Vintage, 1968).

John Sallis, *Crossings: Nietzsche and the Space of Tragedy* (Chicago: The University of Chicago Press, 1991).

Arthur Schopenhauer, *The World as Will and Representation*, tr. E.F.J. Payne (New York: Dover, 1969) vol. II.

M.S. Silk and J.P. Stern, *Nietzsche on Tragedy* (Cambridge: Cambridge University Press, 1981).

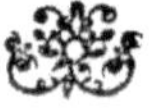

Das griechische Musikdrama
The Greek Music Drama

IN UNSEREM HEUTIGEN Theaterwesen sind nicht nur Erinnerungen und Anklänge an die *dramatischen Künste Griechenlands* aufzufinden: nein, seine *Grundformen* wurzeln auf *hellenischem* Boden, entweder in *natürlichem* Wachsthum oder in Folge einer *künstlichen* Entlehnung. Nur die *Namen* haben sich vielfach verändert und verschoben: ähnlich wie die mittelalterliche Tonkunst die griechischen Tonleitern wirklich noch besaß, auch mit den griechischen Namen, nur daß z.B. das, was die Griechen *„Lokrisch"* nannten, in den Kirchentönen als *„Dorisch"* bezeichnet wird. Ähnliche Verwirrungen begegnen uns auf dem Gebiet der dramatischen Terminologie: das, was der Athener als *„Tragödie"* verstand, werden wir allenfalls unter den Begriff der *„großen Oper"* bringen: wenigstens hat dies Voltaire in einem Brief an den Kardinal Quirini gethan. Dagegen würde ein Hellene in unserer Tragödie fast nichts wiedererkennen, was seiner Tragödie entspräche: wohl aber würde ihm beikommen, daß der ganze Aufbau und der Grundcharakter der Tragödie Shakespeare's seiner sogenannten *neueren Komödie* entnommen sei. Und in der That hat sich aus *ihr*, in ungeheuren Zeiträumen, das römische Drama, das romanisch-germanische Mysterien- und Moralitätenspiel, zuletzt die Tragödie Shakespeare's entfaltet: in ähnlicher Weise, wie in der äußeren Form der *Bühne* Shakespeare's die *genealogische* Verwandtschaft mit der der neueren attischen Komödie nicht verkannt werden darf. Während wir nun hier eine natürlich vorwärtsschreitende, durch Jahrtausende fortgesetzte Entwicklung anzuerkennen haben, ist jene wirkliche Tragödie des Alterthums, das Kunstwerk des Aeschylus und Sophokles, der modernen Kunst willkürlich eingeimpft worden. Das, was wir heute die *Oper* nennen, das Zerrbild des antiken

In our contemporary theater we do not find only memories and echoes of the *dramatic arts of Greece*: rather, its *basic forms* are rooted in *Hellenic* soil, from which they grow *naturally* or to which they are more *artificially* related. Only their *names* have become subject to numerous shifts and changes: just as medieval musicology retained the Greek diatonic scales, along with their names, but what the Greeks, for instance, called "*Locrian*" was known among the Church modes as "*Dorian*."[1] We encounter similar confusions in the field of dramatic terminology: what the Athenians called "*tragedy*" is something which, if we had to find a term, we would call "*Grand Opera*": at least, this is what Voltaire did in a letter to Cardinal Quirini.[2] By contrast, a Greek would recognize in our tragedy almost nothing corresponding to his tragedy; although he would certainly guess that the entire structure and fundamental character of Shakespeare's tragedy is borrowed from what he would call *New Comedy*.[3] In fact, it is from *this* source, after incredible stretches of time, that the Roman drama, the Romanic-Germanic mystery- and morality-play, and finally Shakespearean tragedy, arises: in a similar way as, in its external form, the *genealogical* relationship of Shakespeare's *stage* to that of the New Attic Comedy cannot be overlooked.[4] Whilst we *can* recognize here a development that progresses naturally across the millennia, the genuine tragedy of antiquity, the works of Aeschylus and Sophocles, has been arbitrarily grafted onto modern art.[5] What, today, we call *opera*, the distorted image of the music drama of antiquity, has arisen through a direct mimicry of antiquity:

Musikdrama's, ist durch direkte Nachäffung des Alterthums entstanden: ohne die unbewußte Kraft eines natürlichen Triebes, nach einer abstrakten Theorie gebildet, hat sie sich, wie ein künstlich erzeugter homunculus, als der böse Kobold unserer modernen Musikentwicklung geberdet. Jene vornehmen und gelehrt gebildeten Florentiner, die im Anfange des 17t. Jahrhunderts die Entstehung der Oper veranlaßten, hatten die deutlich ausgesprochne Absicht, *die* Wirkungen der Musik zu erneuern, die sie im Alterthume, nach so vielen beredten Zeugnissen, gehabt habe. Merkwürdig! Schon der erste Gedanke an die Oper war ein Haschen nach Effekt. Durch solche Experimente werden die Wurzeln einer unbewußten, aus dem Volksleben herauswachsenden Kunst abgeschnitten oder mindestens arg verstümmelt. So wurde in Frankreich das volksthümliche Drama durch die sogenannte klassische Tragödie verdrängt, also durch eine rein auf gelehrtem Wege entstandene Gattung, die die Quintessenz des Tragischen, ohne alle Beimischungen, enthalten sollte. Auch in Deutschland ist die natürliche Wurzel des Drama's, das Fastnachtspiel, seit der Reformation untergraben worden; seitdem wurde die Neuschöpfung einer nationalen Form kaum wieder versucht, dagegen nach den vorhandenen Mustern fremder Nationen gedacht und gedichtet. Für die Entwicklung der modernen Künste ist die Gelehrsamkeit, das bewußte Wissen und Vielwissen der eigentliche Hemmschuh: alles Wachsen und Werden im Reiche der Kunst muß in tiefer Nacht vor sich gehen. Die Geschichte der Musik lehrt es, daß die gesunde Weiterentwicklung der *griechischen* Musik im frühen Mittelalter plötzlich auf das stärkste gehemmt und beeinträchtigt wurde, als man in Theorie & Praxis mit Gelehrsamkeit auf das Alte zurückgieng. Das Resultat war eine

without the unconscious force of a natural drive, but formed in accordance with an abstract theory, it has behaved like an artificially produced homunculus, as if it were the evil imp of our modern musical development. Those noble and scholarly Florentines to whom opera owes its origin at the beginning of the seventeenth century had the clearly articulated intention of renewing precisely those musical effects which music, according to numerous eloquent testimonies, had had in antiquity. Remarkable! The first thought concerning opera already involved a striving for effect. Through such experiments the roots of an unconscious art nourished by the life of the people were cut off or at least severely mutilated. Thus, in France, popular drama was displaced by so-called classical tragedy, that is, by a genre that had arisen in a purely scholarly way and supposedly contained the quintessence of tragedy, without any admixture. In Germany, too, the natural root of drama, the Shrovetide play, has been undermined since the Reformation; ever since, the new creation of national form has hardly ever been tried, instead the models of foreign nations govern our thinking and writing. The real obstacle to the development of modern art forms is erudition, conscious knowledge, and an excess of knowledge: all growth and development in the realm of art has to take place in the dead of night. The history of music teaches us that the healthy progressive development of *Greek* music in the early Middle Ages was suddenly blocked and hindered in an extreme way when one used scholarship in theory and practice to return to the age of antiquity. The result was

unglaubliche Verkümmerung des Geschmacks: — — —[2] Es war dies Litteraturmusik, Lesemusik. Was uns hier als helle Absurdität anmuthet, dürfte auf dem Gebiete, das ich besprechen will, wohl nur Wenigen sogleich als solche einleuchten. Ich behaupte nämlich, daß, der uns bekannte Aeschylus und Sophokles uns nur als Textbuchdichter, als Librettisten bekannt sind, das heißt daß sie uns eben unbekannt sind. Während wir nämlich im Bereich der Musik über das gelehrte Schattenspiel einer Lesemusik längst hinaus sind, ist im Gebiete der Poesie die Unnatürlichkeit der Buchdichtung so allein herrschend, daß es Besinnung kostet, sich zu sagen, in wie fern wir gegen Pindar Aeschylus und Sophokles ungerecht sein müssen, ja weshalb wir sie eigentlich nicht kennen. Wenn wir sie als Dichter bezeichnen, so meinen wir eben Buchdichter: gerade damit aber verlieren wir jeden Einblick in ihr Wesen, das uns einzig aufgeht, wenn wir die Oper uns einmal in kräftiger phantasiereicher Stunde so idealisirt vor die Seele führen, daß uns eben die Anschauung des antiken Musikdrama's sich erschließt. Denn so verzerrt auch alle Verhältnisse an der sogenannten großen Oper sind, so sehr sie selbst ein Produkt der Zerstreuung, nicht der Sammlung ist, die Sklavin schlechtester Reimerei und unwürdiger Musik: so sehr hier alles Lüge und Schamlosigkeit ist, immerhin giebt es kein anderes Mittel, über Sophokles sich klar zu werden, als indem wir aus dieser Karikatur das Urbild zu errathen suchen und alles Verbogene und Verzerrte in begeisterter Stunde uns hinwegdenken. Jenes Phantasiebild muß dann sorgfältig untersucht und, seinen einzelnen Theilen nach, mit der Tradition des Alterthums zusammengehalten werden, damit wir nicht etwa das Hellenische überhellenisiren und ein Kunstwerk uns ausdenken, das nirgends in aller

an unbelievable impoverishment of taste: — — —[6] This was literary music, music to be read. What seems to us like an obvious absurdity may well have immediately appeared as such only to a few in the field I wish to discuss. I maintain that Aeschylus and Sophocles are known to us only as textbook-poets, as librettists, which means that we do not know them at all. While in the sphere [*Bereich*] of music we have long gone beyond the scholarly shadow-play of music to be read, in the sphere [*Gebiete*] of poetry the unnaturalness of writing accompanying texts is itself so dominant that it requires considerable effort to tell oneself just how unfair we must be to Pindar, Aeschylus, and Sophocles, which is the reason why we do not really know them. If we call them poets, we mean book-poets: but for precisely that reason we lose the insight into their being that we can only have if we present the *opera* to our mind's eye in a moment of imaginative power and in such an idealized way that we are granted an intuition into the music drama of antiquity. For, however distorted all its relations to so-called grand opera are, and however much it is a product of distraction, rather than concentration, the slave of the poorest rhyming and ignoble music: however much everything connected with it is lies and shamelessness, there is after all no other means of understanding Sophocles than to try to discern the original image in this caricature, excluding from thought in moments of enthusiasm all its distortions and deformations. That fantasy image then has to be carefully examined and, in its individual parts, held up against the tradition of antiquity, so that we do not over-Hellenize the Hellenics and invent a work of art that has never

Welt eine Heimat hat. Das ist keine geringe Gefahr. Galt es doch bis vor nicht lange als unbedingtes Kunstaxiom, daß alle ideale Plastik farblos sein müsse, daß die antike Skulptur die Anwendung der Farbe nicht zulasse. Ganz langsam und unter dem heftigsten Widerstreben jener Hyperhellenen, hat sich die polychrome Anschauung der antiken Plastik Bahn gebrochen, nach der sie nicht mehr nackt, sondern mit einem farbigen Überzug bekleidet gedacht werden muß. In ähnlicher Weise erfreut sich der ästhetische Satz einer allgemeinen Beliebtheit, daß eine Verbindung zweier und mehrerer Künste keine Erhöhung des ästhetischen Genusses erzeugen könne, vielmehr eine barbarische Geschmacksverirrung sei. Dieser Satz aber beweist höchstens die schlechte moderne Gewöhnung, daß wir nicht mehr als ganze Menschen genießen können: wir sind gleichsam durch die absoluten Künste in Stücke zerrissen und genießen nun auch als Stücke, bald als Ohrenmenschen, bald als Augenmenschen usw. Halten wir dagegen, wie der geistvolle Anselm Feuerbach sich jenes antike Drama als Gesammtkunst vorstellt.

„Es ist nicht zu verwundern, sagt er, wenn bei einer tiefbegründeten Wahlverwandtschaft die einzelnen Künste endlich wieder zu einem unzertrennlichen Ganzen, als einer neuen Kunstform sich verschmelzen. Die olympischen Spiele führten die gesonderten Griechenstämme zur politisch religiösen Einheit zusammen: das dramatische Festspiel gleicht einem Wiedervereinigungsfeste der griechischen Künste. Das Vorbild desselben war schon in jenen Tempelfesten gegeben, wo die plastische Erscheinung des Gottes vor einer andächtigen Menge mit Tanz und Gesang gefeiert wurde. Wie dort, so bildet auch hier die Architektur den Rahmen und die Basis, durch welche sich die höhere poetische Sphäre sichtbar gegen

existed anywhere in the world. This is no small danger. After all, until recently it was considered to be an unconditional axiom of art that all idealistic sculpture had to be without color, and that sculpture in antiquity did not permit the use of color. Quite slowly, and encountering the resistance of all those ultra-Hellenists, it has gradually become possible to accept the polychrome view of ancient sculpture, according to which we should no longer imagine that statues were naked, but clothed in a colorful veneer. Similarly, general approval is now given to the aesthetic principle that a union of two or more art forms cannot produce an intensification of aesthetic pleasure, but is rather a barbaric error of taste. But this principle proves above all the bad modern way we have become accustomed to, the idea that we can no longer enjoy as complete human beings: we are, as it were, torn into little pieces by absolute art forms, and hence enjoy as little pieces, in one moment as ear-men, in another as eye-men, & so on.[7] Let us contrast this view with what the brilliant Anselm Feuerbach[8] has to say about the drama of antiquity as a total work of art:

"It is not surprising," he says, "that a profound elective affinity allows the individual art forms to blend together again into an inseparable whole, into a new art form. The Olympic Games brought the separate Greek tribes together into a political and religious unity: the dramatic festival is like a festive reunification of the Greek art forms. The model for this already existed in those temple festivals where the plastic appearance of the god was celebrated in front of a devout audience by means of dance and song. As there, so here architecture constituted the framework and the foundation,

die Wirklichkeit abschließt. An der Scenerie sehen wir den Maler beschäftigt und allen Reiz eines bunten Farbenspiels in der Pracht des Kostüms ausgebreitet. Der Seele des Ganzen hat sich die Dichtkunst bemächtigt; aber diese wieder nicht als einzelne Dichtform, wie im Tempeldienst z.B. als Hymne. Jene dem griechischen Drama so wesentlichen Berichte des Angelos und des Exangelos, oder der handelnden Personen selbst, führen uns in das Epos zurück. Die lyrische Poesie hat in den leidenschaftlichen Scenen und im Chor ihre Stelle und zwar nach allen ihren Abstufungen von dem unmittelbaren Ausbruch des Gefühls in Interjektionen, von der zartesten Blume des Liedes an bis zur Hymne und Dithyrambe hinauf. In Recitation, Gesang und Flötenspiel und dem Taktschritte des Tanzes ist der Ring noch nicht völlig geschlossen. Denn wenn die Poesie das innerste Grundelement des Dramas bildet, so tritt ihr in dieser ihr neuen Form die Plastik entgegen."

Soweit Feuerbach. Sicher ist, daß wir einem solchen Kunstwerke gegenüber erst lernen müßten, wie man als ganzer Mensch zu genießen habe: während es zu befürchten ist, daß man, auch hingestellt vor ein derartiges Werk, es sich in lauter Stücke zerlegen würde, um es sich anzueignen. Ich glaube sogar, daß wer von uns plötzlich in eine athenische Festvorstellung versetzt würde, zunächst den Eindruck eines gänzlich fremdartigen und barbarischen Schauspiels haben würde. Und dies aus sehr vielen Gründen. In hellster Tagessonne, ohne alle die geheimnißvollen Wirkungen des Abends und des Lampenlichts, in grellster Wirklichkeit sähe er einen ungeheuren offnen Raum mit Menschen überfüllt: aller Blicke hingerichtet auf eine in der Tiefe wunderbar sich bewegende maskirte Männerschaar und ein paar übermenschlich große Puppen,

by means of which the higher poetic sphere is visibly separated from reality. We see the painter at work on the backdrop and all the charm of a bright display of color in the magnificence of the costumes. The art of poetry has taken over the soul of the whole; but it has done so, not as a single poetic form, as in the worship of the temple, for instance, as a hymn. The reports of the *angelos* and the *exangelos*,[9] so important for the Greek drama, or of the actors themselves, lead us back to the epic. Lyric poetry has its place in the scenes of passion and in the chorus, in all its various degrees from the unmediated outbreak of feeling in exclamations, from the most delicate blossoming of song up to the hymn and the dithyramb. In recitation and song, in the playing of the flute and in the rhythmic steps of the dance, the circle is not entirely closed. For if poetry is the innermost basic element of the drama, it is in its new form that it meets together with sculpture."[10]

Thus Feuerbach. What is certain is that, when confronted with such a work of art, we have first of all to learn how one enjoys as a complete human being: while it is to be feared that, confronted with such a work, one would take it to pieces, in order to make it one's own.[11] I even believe that if one of us were to be suddenly transported back to an Athenian festival performance, he would have the impression of being at an entirely strange and barbaric spectacle. This would be the case for many different reasons. In the bright light of the daytime sun, without the mysterious effects of evening and the stage lighting, in dazzling reality he would see an enormous open space full to bursting with people: everyone's gaze would be directed towards a crowd of

die auf einem langen schmalen Bühnenraume im langsamsten Zeitmaße auf und niederschreiten. Denn wie anders als Puppen müssen wir jene Wesen nennen, die auf den hohen Stelzen der Kothurne stehend, mit riesenmäßigen den Kopf überragenden stark bemalten Masken vor dem Gesicht, an Brust und Leib, Armen und Beinen bis in das Unnatürliche ausgepolstert und ausgestopft, sich kaum bewegen können, niedergedrückt von der Last eines tief herabfallenden Schleppgewandes und eines mächtigen Kopfputzes. Dabei haben diese Gestalten durch die weit geöffneten Mundlöcher im stärksten Tone zu reden und zu singen, um sich einer Zuschauermasse von mehr als 20,000 Menschen verständlich zu machen: fürwahr, eine Heldenaufgabe, die eines marathonischen Kämpfers würdig ist. Noch größer aber wird unsre Bewunderung, wenn wir vernehmen, daß der Einzelne von diesen Schauspieler-Sängern in 10stündiger Anspannung gegen 1600 Verse von sich zu geben hat, darunter wenigstens sechs größere und kleinere Gesangsstücke. Und dies vor einem Publikum, das jedes Übermaß im Ton, jeden unrichtigen Accent unerbittlich ahndete, in Athen, wo nach Lessings Ausdruck selbst der Pöbel ein feines und zärtliches Urtheil hatte. Welche Koncentration und Übung der Kräfte, welche langwierige Vorbereitung, welchen Ernst und Enthusiasmus im Erfassen der künstlerischen Aufgabe müssen wir hier voraussetzen, kurz, welch ein ideales Schauspielerthum! Hier waren Aufgaben für die edelsten Bürger gestellt, hier entwürdigte sich, auch im Falle des Mißlingens, ein Marathonkämpfer nicht, hier empfand der Schauspieler, wie er in seinem Kostüm eine Erhebung über die alltägliche Menschenbildung darstellte, auch in sich einen Aufschwung, in dem

men below, wearing masks and moving in a wondrous way, and a few superhumanly sized puppets, marching up and down a long, thin stage in slow, regular steps. For what else, other than puppets, would we call those beings, standing on high heels or on *cothurni*, with giant-sized, gaudily painted masks in front of their faces and covering their heads, their chests and bodies, arms and legs padded out and filled with stuffing in an entirely unnatural way, hardly able to move, weighed down by the burden of a trailing cloak and massive headgear. At the same time, these figures have to speak and to sing through the wide open mouth-holes as loudly as possible, in order to be understood by an audience of more than 20,000 people: to be sure, an heroic task, worthy of a marathon contestant. Our admiration will become even greater, however, when we realize that an individual actor-singer has to recite across a ten-hour period some 1600 verses, among them at least six larger and smaller sung set-pieces. And all this in front of a public that unforgivingly punished every slip of pitch, every incorrect emphasis in Athens where, as Lessing put it, even the rabble had a fine and delicate sense of judgment.[12] What concentration and exercise of human forces, what protracted preparation, what seriousness and enthusiasm in the sense of the artistic task we have to presume here, in short, what an ideal concept of the actor! Here tasks were set for the most noble citizens, here a marathon contestant, even in the event of a mistake, suffered no loss of dignity; here the actor, just as he in his costume represented an elevation above the day-to-day level of human beings, experienced an internal sense of uplift, in which the pathos-laden, immensely

die pathetischen, schwerwuchtigen Worte des Aeschylus ihm eine natürliche Sprache sein mußten.

Weihevoll aber gleich dem Schauspieler lauschte auch der *Zuhörer*: auch über ihn breitete sich eine ungewöhnliche langersehnte Feststimmung aus. Nicht die ängstliche Flucht vor der Langeweile, der Wille sich und seine Erbärmlichkeit um jeden Preis für einige Stunden los zu sein, trieb jene Männer ins Theater. Der Grieche flüchtete sich aus der ihm so gewohnten zerstreuenden Öffentlichkeit, aus dem Leben in Markt Straße und Gerichtshalle, in die ruhig stimmende, zur Sammlung einladende Feierlichkeit der Theaterhandlung: nicht wie der alte Deutsche, der Zerstreuung begehrte, wenn er den Cirkel seines innerlichen Daseins einmal zerschnitt, und der die rechte lustige Zerstreuung in der gerichtlichen Wechselrede fand, die deshalb auch für sein Drama Form und Atmosphäre bestimmte. Die Seele des Atheners dagegen, der die Tragödie an den großen Dionysien anzuschauen kam, hatte in sich noch etwas von jenem Element, aus dem die Tragödie geboren ist. Es ist dies der übermächtig hervorbrechende Frühlingstrieb, ein Stürmen und Rasen in gemischter Empfindung, wie es alle naiven Völker und die gesammte Natur beim Nahen des Frühlings kennen. Bekanntlich sind auch unsre Fastnachtsspiele und Maskenscherze ursprünglich solche Frühlingsfeste, die nur aus kirchlichen Anlässen etwas zurückdatiert sind. Hier ist alles tiefster Instinkt: jene ungeheuren dionysischen Schwarmzüge im alten Griechenland haben ihre Analogie in den St. Johann- und St. Veitstänzern des Mittelalters, die in größter, immer wachsender Menge[3] tanzend singend und springend von Stadt zu Stadt zogen. Mag auch die heutige Medicin von jener Erscheinung als von

powerful words of Aeschylus must have seemed like a natural language.

With the same solemnity as the actor the spectator *listened*: over him, too, is spread an unusual, much-longed-for festive mood. It was not the anxious flight from boredom, the will to be rid of one's self and one's misery for a few hours at any cost, that drove these men into the theater. The ancient Greeks took refuge from the familiar distractions of public life, from life in the market-place, the street, and the courts of justice, in the calm and meditation-promoting festivities of theatrical action: not like the German of old, who desired entertainment as soon as he had cut through the circle of his interior existence, and found an amusing source of diversion in the cut-and-thrust of the law courts, which came to determine the form and atmosphere of his drama. By contrast, the soul of the Athenian who came to watch the tragedy at the great Dionysian festivals still bore within himself something of that element from which tragedy had sprung. That is, the powerful drive of springtime when it bursts forth, a storming and raging in a mixture of emotions that is familiar to all naïve peoples and the whole of nature when spring approaches. As is well known, our carnival plays and masquerades were originally just such spring festivals, which have only become unfashionable because of pressure from the Church. Here everything draws on deep instincts: those immense Dionysian processions in ancient Greece find their counterpart in the dancers of St. John and St. Vitus in the Middle Ages, when a crowd, growing ever larger in number, sang and danced its way from town to town.[13] Even if today the medical establishment speaks of this phenomenon as a national

einer Volksseuche des Mittelalters sprechen: wir wollen nur festhalten, daß das antike Drama aus einer solchen Volksseuche erblüht ist, und daß es das Unglück der modernen Künste ist, *nicht* aus solchem geheimnißvollen Quell entflossen zu sein. Es ist nicht etwa Muthwille und willkürliche Ausgelassenheit, wenn in den ersten Anfängen des Dramas wildbewegte Schwärme, als Satyrn und Silene kostümirt, die Gesichter mit Ruß, Mennig und andern Pflanzensäften beschmiert, mit Blumenkränzen auf dem Kopf, durch Feld und Wald schweiften: die allgewaltige, so plötzlich sich kundgebende Wirkung des Frühlings steigert hier auch die Lebenskräfte zu einem solchen Übermaß, daß ekstatische Zustände, Visionen und der Glaube an die eigne Verzauberung allerwärts hervortreten, und gleichgestimmte Wesen schaarenweise durchs Land ziehen. Und hier ist die Wiege des Dramas. Denn nicht damit beginnt dasselbe, daß jemand sich vermummt und bei Anderen eine Täuschung erregen will: nein, vielmehr, indem der Mensch außer sich ist und sich selbst verwandelt und verzaubert glaubt. In dem Zustande des „Außer-sich-seins", der Ecstase, ist nur ein Schritt noch nöthig: wir kehren nicht wieder in uns zurück, sondern gehen in ein anderes Wesen ein, so daß wir uns als Verzauberte geberden. Daher rührt im letzten Grunde das tiefe Erstaunen beim Anblick des Drama's: der Boden wankt, der Glaube an die Unlöslichkeit und Starrheit des Individuums. Und wie der dionysische Schwärmer an seine Verwandlung glaubt, recht im Gegensatz zu Zettel im Sommernachtstraum, so glaubt der dramatische Dichter an die Wirklichkeit seiner Gestalten. Wer diesen Glauben nicht hat, der kann zwar noch zu den Thyrsusschwingern, den Dilettanten gehören, nicht aber zu den rechten Dienern des Dionysos, den Bacchen.

epidemic of the Middle Ages: we should remember that the ancient drama blossomed forth from precisely such a national epidemic, and that it is a misfortune that the arts today do *not* flow from such a mysterious source. Not from willfulness and deliberate exuberance in the first beginnings of the drama did wildly-moving crowds, dressed as satyrs and sileni, their faces smeared with soot, vermilion, and other plant-based pigments, their heads adorned with floral wreaths, roam through field and wood: the all-powerful, so suddenly announced effect of spring here intensifies the powers of life into such an excess that ecstatic conditions, visions, and the belief in one's own enchanted state appear everywhere, and similarly affected individuals stream in hordes across the countryside. And here is the cradle of drama. For drama does not begin when someone disguises himself and seeks to deceive other people: no, rather it begins when a human being steps outside himself and believes himself to be transformed & enchanted. In this condition of "being-outside-of-oneself," or ecstasy, only one further step is necessary: we do not return back into ourselves, but turn into another being, so that we ourselves behave like enchanted beings. This is the fundamental reason for our deep astonishment at the sight of the drama: the ground shakes, the belief in the indissolubility and permanence of the individual. And just as the Dionysian reveler believes in his transformation, in this respect the exact opposite to Bottom in *A Midsummer Night's Dream,*[14] so the dramatic poet believes in the reality of his characters.[15] Whoever does not share this belief can neither belong to the thyrsus-bearers, the dilettantes, nor for that matter to the true followers of Dionysos, the Bacchantes.[16]

Etwas von diesem dionysischen Naturleben war in der Blüthezeit des attischen Dramas auch noch in der Seele der Zuhörer. Das war kein faules fatiguirtes allabendliches Abonnementspublikum, das mit müden abgehetzten Sinnen zum Theater kommt, um sich hier in Emotion versetzen zu lassen. Im Gegensatz zu diesem Publikum, das die Zwangsjacke unseres heutigen Theaterwesens ist, hatte der athenische Zuschauer seine frischen morgendlichen, festlich angeregten Sinne noch, wenn er sich auf den Stufen des Theaters niederließ. Das Einfache war für ihn noch nicht zu einfach: seine ästhetische Gelehrsamkeit bestand in den Erinnerungen an frühere glückliche Theatertage, sein Zutrauen zu dem dramatischen Genius seines Volkes war grenzenlos. Was das Wichtigste aber ist, er schlürfte den Trank der Tragödie so selten, daß er ihn jedesmal wie zum ersten Male genoß. In diesem Sinne will ich das Wort des bedeutendsten lebenden Architekten anführen, der für die Deckengemälde und ausgemalte Kuppeln sein Votum abgiebt. „Nichts ist vortheilhafter, sagt er, für das Kunstwerk als das Entrücktsein aus der vulgären unmittelbaren Berührung mit dem Nächsten und aus der gewohnten Sehlinie des Menschen. Durch die Gewohnheit des Bequemsehen's wird der Sehnerv so abgestumpft, daß er den Reiz und die Verhältnisse der Farben und Formen nur noch wie hinter einem Schleier erkennt." Es wird sicher erlaubt sein, etwas Analoges auch für den seltnen Genuß des Dramas zu beanspruchen: es kommt den Bildern und den Dramen zu Gute, die mit etwas ungewohnter Haltung und Empfindung angeschaut werden: wenn damit auch noch nicht die altrömische Sitte, im Theater zu stehen, anempfohlen werden soll.

Something of this Dionysian life of nature could still be found in the soul of the spectators in the heyday of the Attic drama. It was no tired, lazy audience with a subscription ticket to every performance, arriving with weary and enervated senses in the theater in order to find emotional stimulation. In contrast to this audience, which is the straitjacket of our contemporary theater, the Athenian spectator still had the fresh senses of early morning, albeit now in a festive mood, when he sat down on the steps of the auditorium. What was simple was, for him, not yet too simple. His aesthetic erudition consisted in the memories of previous happy days in the theater, his confidence in the dramatic genius of his people knew no limits. Most important, however, was that he drank the potion of tragedy so rarely that, every time he did, he enjoyed it as he had the first time. It is in this sense that I wish to cite the words of the most important living architect who has passed his judgment on ceiling paintings and painted domes: "Nothing is more advantageous," he says, "for the work of art than when it is beyond any immediate and vulgar contact with what is close at hand or seen from the usual perspective of human beings. Through becoming accustomed to seeing things easily, the optic nerve becomes so stunted, that it can only recognize the stimulus and the relations between colors and forms as if behind a veil."[17] Beyond a doubt something analogous can be claimed about enjoying a drama only rarely: it is to the advantage of pictures and plays when they are seen from an unusual angle and perceived differently: without going so far as to recommend the ancient Roman practice of standing in the theater.

Wir haben bis jetzt nur den Schauspieler und den Zuschauer in's Auge gefaßt. Denken wir zu dritt auch an den Poeten: und zwar fasse ich hier das Wort in seinem weitesten Sinne, so wie es die Griechen verstanden. Es ist richtig, daß die griechischen Tragiker ihre unermeßlichen Einwirkungen auf die neuere Kunst nur als Librettisten geübt haben: wenn das aber wahr ist, so lebe ich der Überzeugung, daß eine wirkliche und ganze Vergegenwärtigung einer äschyleischen Trilogie, mit attischen Schauspielern, Publikum und Poeten, auf uns geradezu eine zerschmetternde Wirkung thun müßte, weil sie uns den künstlerischen Menschen in einer Vollkommenheit und Harmonie offenbaren würde, gegen die unsre großen Dichter gleichsam als schön begonnene, doch nicht zu Ende gearbeitete Statuen erscheinen möchten.

Die Aufgabe war im griechischen Alterthum für den Dramatiker so schwer als möglich gestellt: eine Freiheit, wie sie unsere Bühnendichter nach Wahl des Stoffs, der Schauspielerzahl und unzähliger Dinge genießen, würde dem attischen Kunstrichter als Zuchtlosigkeit erschienen sein. Durch die gesammte griechische Kunst geht das stolze Gesetz, daß nur das Schwerste eine Aufgabe für den freien Mann ist. So hieng die Autorität und der Ruhm eines plastischen Kunstwerkes sehr von der Schwierigkeit der Bearbeitung, der Härte des verwendeten Stoffes ab. Zu den besonderen Schwierigkeiten, vermöge deren der Weg zur dramatischen Berühmtheit niemals ein sehr breiter geworden ist, gehört die beschränkte Zahl der Schauspieler, die Verwendung des Chors, der begrenzte Mythenkreis, vor allem aber jene Fünfkämpfertugend, die Nothwendigkeit, als Dichter und Musiker, in der Orchestik und der Regie, zuletzt als Schauspieler produktiv begabt zu sein. Das was für unsre dramatischen

Thus far we have only considered the actor & the spectator. Let us think, thirdly, of the poet: and here I am using the word in its widest sense, as the Greeks understood it. It is true that the Greek tragedians have exercised their immeasurable influence on more recent art only as librettists: but if that is true, I am nevertheless convinced that a complete, authentic presentation of an Aeschylean trilogy, with Attic actors, audience, and poets, would have on us a shattering effect, because it would reveal to us the artistic human being in such perfection and harmony that in comparison our own great writers would appear like statues which are beautiful in their inception but are never completed.

In Greek antiquity, the dramatist was confronted with a task that was made as difficult as possible: the freedom to choose material, the number of actors, and innumerable other things that our dramatists enjoy, would have struck an Attic critic as a lack of discipline. Throughout the whole of Greek art one finds the proud law that only what is most difficult is a fit task for a free man. And so the authority and reputation of a sculptural work of art depended greatly on the difficulty of its working, or on the hardness of the material used. Among the particular difficulties, thanks to which the path to dramatic fame has never been a wide one, are the limited number of actors, the use of the chorus, the limited cycle of myths, but, above all, that virtue of the pentathlon athlete, the necessity to be productively talented as a writer and a musician, as a conductor and a director, and finally as an actor. For our dramatists, their lifeboat is the novelty, and thus

Dichter immer der Rettungsanker ist, das ist die Neuheit und damit das Interessante ihres Stoffes, den sie für ihr Drama gewählt haben. Sie denken, wie die italienischen Improvisatoren, die eine neue Geschichte bis zu ihrem Höhe- punkt und zur höchsten Steigerung der Spannung erzählen und dann überzeugt sind, daß niemand mehr vor Schluß davongeht. Das Festhalten bis zum Schluß durch den Reiz des Interessanten war nun bei den griechischen Tragikern etwas Unerhörtes: die Stoffe ihrer Meisterwerke waren altbekannt und in epischer und lyrischer Form den Zuhörern von Kindheit an vertraut. Es war bereits eine Heldenthat für einen Orest und einen Ödipus wahrhafte Theilnahme zu erwecken: aber wie beschränkt, wie eigensinnig eingeengt waren die Mittel, die zur Erregung dieser Theilnahme gebraucht werden durften! Hier kommt vor allem der Chor in Betracht, der für den antiken Dichter ebenso wichtig war wie für den französischen Tragiker die vornehmen Personen, die zu beiden Seiten der Scene ihre Sitze hatten und die Bühne gewissermaßen in ein fürstliches Vorzimmer verwandelten. Wie der französische Tragiker diesem sonderbaren nicht mitspielenden und doch mitspielenden „Chor" zu liebe die Dekorationen nicht ändern durfte, wie sich Sprache und Geste auf der Bühne nach ihm modelte: so verlangte der antike Chor für die ganze Handlung in jedem Drama Öffentlichkeit der Handlung, den freien Platz als die Aktionsstätte der Tragödie. Dies ist eine verwegene Forderung: denn die tragische That und die Vorbereitung zu ihr pflegt sich gerade nicht auf der Straße finden zu lassen, sondern erwächst am Besten in der Verborgenheit. Alles öffentlich, alles im hellen Licht, alles in Gegenwart des Chors — das war die grausame Forderung. Nicht daß man aus irgend einer ästhetischen Spitzfindigkeit dies

the allure of their material, which they have chosen for their play. They think in the same way as Italian improvisation artists do: they narrate a new story to its climax and to the highest point of excitement, and then are convinced that no one will leave before the end. To keep hold of one's audience right to the end by stimulating interest was, to the Greek tragedians, something unheard-of: the subject-matter of their masterpieces was already well-known and, in epic and lyric form alike, deeply familiar to each audience member from his childhood. It was already an heroic deed to awaken genuine ruth for an Orestes, for an Oedipus: but how limited, how obstinately restricted were the means that could be used to arouse this ruth! In this respect, the only thing that matters is the chorus, which for ancient playwrights was as important as the noble characters, seated on either side of the stage in a way that transformed it into a royal antechamber, were for the French tragedians. Just as, for the sake of this curious, non-participatory and nevertheless participatory "chorus," the French tragedian was not allowed to change the scenery, and just as language and gesture on the stage modeled themselves accordingly: so the ancient chorus demanded that the entire action in each drama take place in public, so that the open square was the place of action for the tragedy. This is an audacious demand: for the tragic deed and the events leading up to it tend not to take place on the open street, but rather to grow in secret. Everything made public, everything in daylight, everything in the presence of the chorus — this was the cruel demand. Not that, out of any kind of aesthetic fastidiousness, this was any-

irgendwann einmal als Forderung ausgesprochen hätte: vielmehr war in dem langen Entwicklungsprozeß des Dramas diese Stufe erreicht worden, und man hatte sie festgehalten mit dem Instinkt, daß hier für den tüchtigen Genius eine tüchtige Aufgabe zu lösen sei. Es ist ja bekannt, daß ursprünglich die Tragödie nichts als ein großer Chorgesang war: diese historische Erkenntniß giebt aber in der That den Schlüssel zu jenem wunderlichen Problem. Die Haupt- und Gesammtwirkung der antiken Tragödie beruhte in der besten Zeit immer noch auf dem Chore: er war der Faktor, mit dem vor allem gerechnet werden mußte, den man nicht bei Seite lassen durfte. Jene Stufe, in der sich das Drama ungefähr von Aeschylus bis Euripides hielt, ist die, in der der Chor soweit zurückgedrängt war, um eben gerade noch die Gesammtfärbung anzugeben. Noch ein einziger Schritt weiter und die Scene herrschte über die Orchestra, die Kolonie über die Mutterstadt; die Dialektik der Bühnenpersonen und ihre Einzelgesänge traten vor und überwältigten den bisher gültigen chorisch- musikalischen Gesammteindruck. Dieser Schritt ist gethan worden, und der Zeitgenosse desselben, Aristoteles, fixierte ihn in seiner berühmten, viel verwirrenden, das Wesen des äschyleischen Dramas gar nicht treffenden Definition.

Der erste Gedanke also beim Entwurfe einer dramatischen Dichtung mußte sein, eine Gruppe von Männern oder Frauen zu erdenken, die mit den handelnden Personen eng verbunden sind: sodann mußten Anlässe gesucht werden, bei denen lyrisch-musikalische Massenstimmungen zum Ausbruch kommen konnten. Der Dichter sah gewissermaßen vom Chor aus nach den Bühnenpersonen, und mit ihm das athenische Publikum:

where declared to be a demand: rather, in the long process of its development this stage of the drama had been reached, and had been preserved through the instinct that here, for the veritable genius, was a worthy task to be performed. It is well known that, originally, the tragedy was nothing other than a giant choral-song: this historical insight, however, provides the key to that other curious problem. The main effect and the overall impact of ancient tragedy at its height could still be found in the chorus: it was the chief factor with which one had to contend and which could not be placed to one side. The stage in the development of drama, lasting more or less from Aeschylus to Euripides, is the one where the chorus had been pushed so far into the background that it could barely provide the general tenor. One step further and the action on the stage dominated the orchestra, the colony the founding city, as it were; the dialectical relationship between the actors on the stage and their individual songs came to the fore and overwhelmed the overall choral or musical impression that had hitherto been dominant. This step was indeed taken, and its contemporary, Aristotle, fixed it permanently in his famous, and highly confusing, definition that did not apply at all to the essence of the Aeschylean tragedy.[18]

So the first thought in designing a dramatic text must be to conceive a group of men or women with whom the figures on the stage are closely related: then, one must look for opportunities for the lyrical or musical group feelings to be expressed. To a certain extent the poet looked at the stage characters from the perspective of the chorus, and so did the Athenian audience:

wir, die wir nur das libretto haben, sehen von der Bühne aus nach dem Chor. Die Bedeutung desselben iſt nicht mit einem Gleichniß zu erschöpfen. Wenn Schlegel ihn als den „idealischen Zuschauer" bezeichnet hat, so will das doch nur sagen, daß der Dichter in der Art, wie der Chor die Ereignisse auffaßt, zugleich andeutet, wie nach seinem Wunsche sie der Zuschauer auffassen solle. Damit iſt aber doch nur eine Seite richtig hervorgehoben: vor allem iſt wichtig, daß der Heldenſpieler durch ihn wie durch ein Schallrohr seine Empfindungen in einer kolossalen Vergrößerung dem Zuschauer zuschreit. Obschon eine Mehrheit von Personen, ſtellt er doch musikalisch keine Masse vor, sondern nur ein ungeheures, mit übernatürlicher Lunge begabtes Einzelwesen. Es iſt nicht am Orte darauf hinzuweisen, welcher ethische Gedanke in der unisonen Chormusik der Griechen liegt: die den ſtärkſten Gegensatz zur chriſtlichen Musikentwicklung bildet, in der die Harmonie, das eigentliche Symbol der Mehrheit, lange Zeit so dominirt, daß die Melodie ganz erſtickt war und erſt wieder entdeckt werden mußte. Der Chor iſt es, der die Grenzen der in der Tragödie sich erweisenden Dichterphantasie vorgeschrieben hat: der religiöse Chortanz mit seinem feierlichen Andante umschränkte den sonſt so übermüthigen Erfindungsgeiſt der Dichter: während die englische Tragödie, ohne eine solche Schranke, mit ihrem phantaſtischen Realismus sich viel ungeſtümer, dionysischer, aber doch im Grunde wehmüthiger geberdet, ungefähr wie ein Beethovensches Allegro. Daß der Chor mehrere große Gelegenheiten zu lyrisch-pathe-tischen Kundgebungen hatte, das iſt eigentlich der wichtigſte Satz in der Ökonomie des alten Dramas. Dies iſt aber leicht auch in dem kürzeſten Theilſtück der Sage erreicht: und deshalb fehlt durchaus alles

we, who have only the libretto, look at the chorus from the perspective of the stage. So the significance of this cannot be exhausted with an analogy. When Schlegel called the chorus the "ideal spectator,"[19] this only means that the poet is trying to show in the way the chorus responds to the action how he would like the spectator to respond. But this is to emphasize just one aspect: above all it is important that the actor playing the hero declaims through the chorus as if through a speaking trumpet [*Schallrohr*][20] his feelings to the spectator in hugely expanded form. Although a plurality of persons, musically the chorus does not represent a collective, but an enormous single being endowed with oversized lungs. This is not the place to point out that an ethical idea is associated with the unison choral music of the Greeks, which stands in a strong contrast to the development of Christian music, in which harmony, the true symbol of a collective, dominates for such a long time that the melody became entirely suppressed and recently had to be rediscovered. It was the chorus that laid down the limits to how poetic fantasy revealed itself in tragedy: the religious choral dance with its festive *andante* restrained the otherwise so high-spirited inventive mind of the poets, while the English tragedy, knowing no such bounds, behaved itself in its imaginative realism in a much more impetuous, Dionysian, but basically much more melancholy way, rather like an *allegro* by Beethoven. To give the chorus a number of great opportunities for lyrical, emotional declarations, this is the most important principle in the economy of the ancient drama. This is easily achieved, however, in even the briefest fragment of a saga: hence, the absence

Verwickelte, alles Intriguenhafte, alles fein und künstlich Kombinirte, kurz alles das, was gerade den Charakter des modernen Trauerspiels ausmacht. Im antiken Musikdrama gab es nichts, was man hätte ausrechnen müssen: auch die Schlauheit einzelner Helden des Mythus hat in ihm etwas Einfach-ehrliches an sich. Niemals, auch nicht bei Euripides ist das Wesen des Schauspiels in das des Schachspiels umgewandelt: während allerdings das Schachspielartige zum Grundzug der sogenannten neueren Komödie geworden ist. Deshalb gleichen die einzelnen Dramen der Alten, ihrem einfachen Aufbau nach, einem *einzigen* Akte unserer Tragödien und zwar am meisten dem fünften Akte, der in kurzen raschen Schritten zur Kata- strophe führt. Die französische klassische Tragödie mußte, weil sie ihr Vorbild, das griechische Musikdrama, eben nur als libretto kannte, und mit der Einführung des Chors in Verlegenheiten gerieth, ein ganz neues Element in sich aufnehmen, nur um die von Horaz vorgeschriebnen 5 Akte auszufüllen: dieser Ballast, ohne den sich jene Kunstform nicht auf die See wagen mochte, war die Intrigue, d.h. eine Räthselaufgabe für den Verstand und eine Tummelstätte der *kleinen*, im Grunde untragischen Leidenschaften: womit sich ihr Charakter dem der neuen attischen Komödie bedeutend näherte. Die alte Tragödie war, mit ihr verglichen, arm an Handlung und Spannung: man kann sogar sagen, daß es auf ihren früheren Entwicklungsstufen gar nicht auf das Handeln das *δρᾶμα* abgesehn war, sondern auf das Leiden das *πάθος*. Die Handlung trat erst hinzu, als der Dialog entstand: und alles wahrhafte und ernste Thun wurde auch in der Blüthezeit des Dramas nicht auf offner Scene vorgeführt. Was war die Tragödie ursprünglich anders als eine objek-

of everything that is complicated, of everything that has to do with intrigue, of everything neatly and artificially combined, or in short, everything that defines the character of the modern tragic drama. In the ancient music drama, there was nothing that one would have had to figure out: even the cunning of individual heroes in myths has something simple, something honorable about it. Never, not even in Euripides, is the essence of the drama transformed into a game of chess: while, to be sure, something of the game of chess has become the chief characteristic of the so-called new comedy. For this reason, the entire dramas of the ancient writers, in their simple structure, are like *one* act of our tragedies and resemble most closely the fifth act that leads in short, quick steps to the catastrophe. French classical tragedy, because it knew its predecessor, the Greek music drama, only as a libretto, and had difficulties with the introduction of the chorus, had to take an entirely new element into itself, if only in order to fill out the fifth act as prescribed by Horace:[21] this ballast, without which this art form did not dare to set sail, was the intrigue, i.e., a puzzle for the understanding and a playground for the *small*, essentially non-tragic passions: as a result of which its character came significantly closer to that of the new Attic comedies. Ancient tragedy was, in comparison, poor in action and tension: one could even say that, in its earlier developmental stages, it was not interested at all in action, in δρᾶμα [*drama*], but in suffering, in πάθος [*pathos*]. The plot was only added when the dialogue arose: and every genuine and serious deed took place off-stage in the prime of the drama. What was the tragedy originally other than an objective

tive Lyrik, ein Lied aus dem Zustande bestimmter mythologischer Wesen heraus gesungen, und zwar im Kostüm derselben. Zuerst mußte ein dithyrambischer Chor von zu Satyrn und Silenen verkleideten Männern selbst zu verstehen geben, was ihn in solche Aufregung versetzt habe: er deutete hin auf einen den Zuhörern schnell verständlichen Zug aus der Kampf- und Leidensgeschichte des Dionysos. Später wurde die Gottheit selbst eingeführt, zu einem doppelten Zwecke: einmal um persönlich von seinen Abenteuern zu erzählen, in denen er eben darin steckt und durch die sein Gefolge zu lebhaftester Theilnahme erregt wird. Andernseits ist Dionysos während jener leidenschaftlichen Chorgesänge gewissermaßen das lebende Bild, die lebende Statue des Gottes: und in der That hat der antike Schauspieler etwas vom steinernen Gast bei Mozart. Ein neuerer Musikschriftsteller macht hierüber folgende richtige Bemerkung.

„In unserem kostümirten Schauspieler, sagt er, tritt uns ein natür-licher Mensch, den Griechen trat in der tragischen Maske ein künstlicher, wenn man will, heroisch stylisirter entgegen. Unsere tiefen Bühnen, auf denen oft an hundert Personen gruppiert sind, machen die Darstellungen zu farbigen *Gemälden*, so lebendig sie nur sein können. Die schmale antike Bühne, mit der nahe vorgerückten Hinterwand, machte die wenigen, sich gemessen bewegenden Figuren zu lebenden Basreliefs oder belebten Marmorbildern eines Tempelgiebels. Hätte ein Wunder jenen Marmorgestalten des Streites zwischen Athene und Poseidon im Parthenongiebel Leben eingehaucht, sie würden wohl die Sprache des Sophokles gesprochen haben."

Ich kehre zu dem vorhin angedeuteten Gesichtspunkte zurück, daß im griechischen Drama der Accent auf dem

lyric, a song that was sung from the condition of certain mythological beings, and moreover in their costume? First of all, a dithyrambic chorus, composed of men disguised as satyrs and sileni, had to make what had put it into such a state of excitement: it pointed, in a way that was immediately comprehensible to the spectators, to an episode from the story of the struggles and sufferings of Dionysos. Later, the divinity itself was introduced, for a dual purpose: for one thing, in order to relate in a personal way his adventures, in which he was involved and which aroused his followers into animated participation. For another, during those passionate choral songs Dionysos is, as it were, the living image, the living statue of the god: indeed, the actor of antiquity had something of the stone guest in Mozart.[22] On this matter a music critic has recently made a pertinent observation:

"In the way our actors are costumed," he says, "we see a naturalistic human being, but the ancient Greeks saw in the tragic mask someone artificial, or someone stylized into a hero. Our deep-set stages, on which often up to a hundred people are grouped, turn the performance into colorful *paintings*, as lively as they can be. The narrow stage of ancient times, with its back-stage wall brought forward, turned the few figures, moving with measured steps, into living bas-reliefs or animated marble statues of a temple pediment. If, through a miracle, the marble figures of the dispute between Athena and Poseidon on the pediment of the Parthenon were to be brought to life, they would speak in the language of Sophocles."[23]

Let me return to the point, already made, that in the Greek drama the emphasis was on suffering, not

Erleiden, nicht auf dem Handeln ruht: jetzt wird es leichter sein zu begreifen, weshalb ich meine, daß wir gegen Aeschylus und Sophokles ungerecht sein *müssen*, daß wir sie eigentlich nicht *kennen*. Wir haben nämlich keinen Maßstab, das Urtheil des attischen Publikums über ein Dichterwerk zu controlieren, weil wir nicht wissen oder nur zum geringsten Theile wissen, wie das Erleiden, überhaupt das Gefühlsleben in seinen Ausbrüchen, zum ergreifenden Eindrucke gebracht wurde. Wir sind einer griechischen Tragödie gegenüber incompetent, weil ihre Hauptwirkung zu einem guten Theil auf einem Element beruhte, das uns verloren gegangen ist, auf der Musik. Für die Stellung der Musik zum alten Drama gilt vollkommen, was Gluck in der berühmten Vorrede zu seiner Alceste als Forderung ausspricht. Die Musik sollte die Dichtung unterstützen, den Ausdruck der Gefühle und das Interesse der Situationen verstärken, ohne die Handlung zu unterbrechen oder durch unnütze Verzierungen zu stören. Sie sollte für die Poesie das sein, was die Lebhaftigkeit der Farben und eine glückliche Mischung von Schatten und Licht für eine fehlerfreie und wohlgeordnete Zeichnung sind, welche nur dazu dienen, die Figuren zu beleben, ohne die Umrisse zu zerstören. Die Musik ist also durchaus nur als Mittel zum Zweck verwendet worden: ihre Aufgabe war es, das Erleiden des Gottes und des Helden in stärkstes Mitleiden bei den Zuhörern umzusetzen. Nun hat ja auch das Wort dieselbe Aufgabe, aber es wird ihm viel schwerer und nur auf Umwegen möglich, dieselbe zu lösen. Das Wort wirkt zunächst auf die Begriffswelt und von da aus erst auf die Empfindung, ja häufig genug erreicht es, bei der Länge des Wegs, sein Ziel gar nicht. Die Musik dagegen trifft das Herz unmittelbar, als die wahre allgemeine Sprache, die man überall versteht.

on action: now it will be easier to understand why I believe that we are *necessarily* unfair to Aeschylus and to Sophocles, and that we do not, in fact, really *know* them. For we do not possess a touchstone to assess the judgment of an Attic audience about a literary work, because we do not know, or barely know, how suffering, or how the emotional life as it erupts, was turned into such a moving impression. We lack the competence to deal with a Greek tragedy, because its main effect relies to a large extent on an element that we have lost: on the music. To the place of music in ancient drama one can fully apply the demand expressed by Gluck in his famous preface to his *Alceste*.[24] The music should support the poetic text, intensify the expression of feelings and the interest of the dramatic situation, without interrupting the action or distracting through pointless ornamentation. It should be to poetry what the brightness of colors and a happy combination of shadow and light are for a flawless and well-composed drawing, when they only serve to bring the figures to life without destroying the overall outlines. Music was then used purely as a means to an end: its task was to convert the suffering of the god and the hero into the strongest possible ruth in the spectators. Now, it is true that language also has this task, but it is much more difficult for it to achieve it, and it can only do so by indirect means. Language has an impact primarily on the conceptual world, and only secondarily on the emotions, and frequently it does not, because of the length of the path, reach its goal at all. Music, however, immediately strikes the heart, as the true universal language that is understood everywhere.

Freilich findet man noch jetzt über die griechische Musik Ansichten verbreitet, als ob sie am allerwenigsten eine solche allgemein verständliche Sprache gewesen sei, sondern vielmehr eine auf gelehrtem Wege erfundene, aus akustischen Lehren abstrahirte, uns gänzlich fremdartige Tonwelt bedeute. Man trägt sich hier und da z.B. noch mit dem Aberglauben, in der griechischen Musik sei die große Terz als ein Mißklang empfunden worden. Von solchen Vorstellungen muß man sich gänzlich frei machen und sich immer vorhalten, daß unserem Gefühl die Musik der Griechen viel näher steht als die des Mittelalters. Was uns von alten Kompositionen erhalten ist, erinnert in seiner scharfen rhythmischen Gliederung durchaus an unsere Volkslieder: aus dem Volkslied aber ist die gesammte antike Dichtkunst und Musik hervorgewachsen. Zwar giebt es auch reine Instrumentalmusik: doch machte sich in ihr nur das Virtuosen- thum geltend. Der echte Grieche empfand bei ihr immer etwas Unheimisches, etwas aus der asiatischen Fremde Importirtes. Die eigentlich griechische Musik ist durchaus Vokalmusik: das natürliche Band der Wort- und Tonsprache ist noch nicht zerrissen: und dies bis zu dem Grade, daß der Dichter nothwendig auch der Komponist seines Liedes war. Die Griechen lernten ein Lied gar nicht anders kennen, als durch den Gesang: sie empfanden aber auch beim Anhören das innigste Eins-sein von Wort und Ton. Wir, die wir unter dem Einflusse der modernen Kunstunart, der Vereinzelung der Künste, aufgewachsen sind, sind kaum mehr im Stande, Text und Musik zusammen zu genießen. Wir haben uns eben gewöhnt, getrennt zu genießen, den Text bei der Lektüre — weshalb wir unserem Urtheil nicht trauen, wenn wir ein Gedicht vorlesen, ein Drama vorspielen sehen und nach dem Buch verlangen

Admittedly, one still finds views expressed about Greek music, as if it were the very opposite of such a universally comprehensible language, but rather represented a totally alien world of sound, contrived by scholarly methods, and based on abstract doctrines of acoustics. Every now and then people still think, e.g., about the superstition that in Greek music the major third was considered dissonance. One has to free oneself entirely from such ideas and always remember that the music of the Greeks is much closer to our feeling than the music of the Middle Ages. What has survived of ancient compositions is reminiscent in its strict rhythmic structure of our folk songs: but it is from the folk-song that the entire poetic art and music of antiquity blossomed. Although there is music that is purely instrumental: but it is only an opportunity to display virtuosity. The true Greek always felt such music to be something foreign, imported from Asiatic lands overseas. Genuine Greek music is inherently vocal music: the natural link between the language of words and the language of sounds has not yet been torn apart: and this is true to the extent that the poet was necessarily also the composer of his song. The Greeks learned a song through no other means than singing it: for they sensed when listening the innermost unity of word and sound. But we, who have grown up under the influence of the bad habits of modern art and of its separation of the art forms, are no longer able to enjoy words and music together. For we have got used to enjoying each separately, literature only when reading it — which is why we do not trust our own judgment when a poem is read or a play is acted out, and demand to see the

— und die Musik beim Anhören. Auch finden wir den absurdesten Text erträglich, wenn nur die Musik schön ist: etwas, was einem Griechen so recht eigentlich als Barbarei vorkommen würde.

Außer der eben betonten Schwesterschaft von Poesie und Tonkunst ist für die antike Musik noch zweierlei charakteristisch, ihre Einfachheit, ja Armuth in der Harmonie, ihr Reichthum an rhythmischen Ausdrucksmitteln. Ich habe schon angedeutet, daß der Chorgesang sich vom Sologesang nur durch die Zahl der Stimmen unterschied, und daß nur den begleitenden Instrumenten eine sehr beschränkte Vielstimmigkeit, also Harmonie in unserm Sinne gestattet war. Die aller erste Forderung war, daß man den Inhalt des vorgetragnen Liedes *verstand*: und wenn man ein pindarisches oder äschyleisches Chorlied mit seinen verwegnen Metaphern und Gedankensprüngen wirklich verstand: so setzt dies eine erstaunliche Kunst des Vortrags und zugleich eine äußerst charakteristische musikalische Accentuation und Rhythmik voraus. Dem musikalisch-rhythmischen Periodenbau, der sich im strengsten Parallelismus mit dem Text bewegte, lief nun andernseits, als äußerliches Ausdrucksmittel, die Tanzbewegung zur Seite, die Orchestik. In den Evolutionen der Choreuten, die sich vor den Augen der Zuschauer wie Arabesken auf der breiten Fläche der Orchestra hinzeichneten, empfand man die gewissermaßen sichtbar gewordne Musik. Während die Musik die Wirkung der Dichtung steigerte, so erklärte die Orchestik die Musik. Es erwuchs somit für den Dichter und Tondichter zugleich noch die Aufgabe, ein produktiver Balletmeister zu sein.

Hier ist noch ein Wort über die Grenzen der Musik im Drama zu sagen. Die tiefere Bedeutung dieser Gren-

text — and music when listening to it. We also find the most absurd text to be tolerable, as long as the music is beautiful: something that would seem to a Greek to be truly barbaric.

Beside the sisterly relation just emphasized between poetry and music, two further things are characteristic of ancient music: its simplicity, even poverty, in harmony, its richness in rhythmic means of expression. I have already indicated that the choral song differed from the solo song only in the number of voices, and that the accompanying instruments were permitted only a very limited plurality of voices, or harmony in our sense. The very first demand was that one *understood* the content of the song as it was recited: and if one could really understand a Pindaric or an Aeschylean chorus-song, with its audacious metaphors and its way of leaping from one idea to another, then this implies a remarkable art of recitation and, at the same time, an extremely idiosyncratic musical accentuation and rhythm. To the musical and rhythmic periodic structure, which moved in strict parallel to the text, there corresponded on the other hand, as an external means of expression, the movement of dance on one side, the orchestral dancing. In the evolutions of the choral dances, which are painted before the eyes of the spectators like arabesques on the broad surfaces of the orchestra, one perceived that music had, in a sense, become visible.[25] As the music intensified the effect of the lyrics, so the orchestral dancing articulated the music. Thus the task emerged for the poet and the composer alike to become a creative choreographer.

At this point one should say a further word about the limitations of music in the drama. The deeper sig-

zen als der Achillesferse des antiken Musikdramas, insofern an ihnen sein Zersetzungsprozeß beginnt, soll heute nicht erörtert werden, da ich den Verfall der antiken Tragödie und damit auch den eben angeregten Punkt in meinem nächsten Vortrag zu besprechen gedenke. Hier genüge nur die Thatsache: nicht alles was gedichtet war, konnte gesungen werden, und mitunter wurde auch, wie in unserem Melodram, gesprochen, unter der Begleitung der Instrumentalmusik. Aber jenes Sprechen haben wir uns immer als Halbrecitativ vorzustellen, so daß der ihm eigenthümliche dröhnende Ton keinen Dualismus in das Musikdrama brachte: vielmehr war auch in der Sprache der dominierende Einfluß der Musik mächtig geworden. Man hat eine Art Nachklang dieses Recitativ-Tons in dem sogenannten Lektionston, mit welchem in der katholischen Kirche die Evangelien, die Episteln, manche Gebete vorgetragen werden. „Der lesende Priester macht bei den Interpunktionen und Schlüssen der Sätze gewisse Flexionen der Stimme, wodurch die Deutlichkeit des Vortrags gesichert und zugleich Monotonie vermieden wird. Aber bei wichtigen Momenten der heiligen Handlung hebt sich die Stimme des Geistlichen, das pater noster, die Präfation, der Segen wird zum deklamatorischen Gesänge." Überhaupt erinnert in dem Rituale des Hochamtes vieles an das griechische Musikdrama, nur daß in Griechenland alles viel heller sonniger überhaupt schöner war, dafür auch weniger innerlich und ohne jene räthselvolle unendliche Symbolik der christlichen Kirche.

Hiermit bin ich, geehrteste Versammlung, zum Schluß gekommen. Ich verglich vorhin den Schöpfer des antiken Musikdrama's mit dem Pentathlos, dem Fünfkämpfer:

nificance of these limitations as the Achilles' heel of the ancient music drama, inasmuch as it is here that its process of decline begins, is not going to be discussed today, because I intend to discuss the decline of ancient tragedy, and with that also the point just raised, in my next lecture.[26] For now, this fact should suffice: not everything that had been written could be sung, and sometimes, as in our melodramas, a text was spoken to the accompaniment of instrumental music. But we should always think of that kind of speaking as delivered in a quasi-recitative style, so that the booming tone peculiar to it did not introduce a dualism into the music drama, but also in language, the dominating influence of music had become powerful. A kind of echo of this recitative style can be heard in the so-called "reading tone" used in the Catholic Church to recite the Gospels, the Epistles, and some prayers. "The priest who is reading makes certain inflexions of his voice to indicate the punctuation and the conclusion of sentences, which assures the clarity of the recitation and at the same time avoids monotony. But at important moments of the sacred action the voice of the priest is raised: the *pater noster*, the Preface, the blessing turn into a declamatory chant."[27] The ritual of the High Mass recalls indeed much of the Greek music drama, with the exception that, in Greece, everything was much brighter, more sunlit, altogether more beautiful, but correspondingly less introverted and lacking the mysterious, unending symbolism of the Christian Church.

At this point, dear listeners, I have reached my conclusion. Earlier I compared the creator of the ancient music drama with the pentathlos, the pentathlete:

ein anderes Bild wird uns die Bedeutung eines solchen musikdramatischen Fünfkämpfers für die gesammte alte Kunst näher bringen. Für die Geschichte der antiken Bekleidung hat Aeschylus eine außerordentliche Bedeutung, insofern er den freien Faltenwurf, die Zierlichkeit Pracht und Anmuth des Hauptgewandes einführte, während vor ihm die Griechen in ihrer Kleidung barbarisirten und den freien Faltenwurf nicht kannten. Das griechische Musikdrama ist für die gesammte alte Kunst jener freie Faltenwurf: alles Unfreie, alles Isolirte der einzelnen Künste ist mit ihm überwunden: bei ihrem gemeinsamen Opferfeste werden der Schönheit *und* zugleich der Kühnheit Hymnen gesungen. Gebundenheit und doch Anmuth, Mannichfaltigkeit und doch Einheit, viele Künste in höchster Thätigkeit und doch *ein* Kunstwerk — das ist das antike Musikdrama. Wer aber bei seinem Anblick an das Ideal des jetzigen Kunstreformators erinnert wird, der wird sich zugleich sagen müssen, daß jenes Kunstwerk der Zukunft durchaus nicht etwa eine glänzende, doch täuschende Luftspiegelung ist: was wir von der Zukunft erhoffen, das war schon einmal Wirklichkeit — in einer mehr als zweitausendjährigen Vergangenheit.

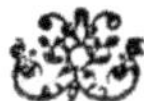

another image will make more accessible to us the significance of such a musical-dramatic pentathlete for the entire art of antiquity. In the history of the ancient costume, Aeschylus has an extraordinary significance, inasmuch as he introduced the free arrangement of the folds, the delicateness, magnificence, and grace of the main robe, while previously the Greeks looked like barbarians in their costumes and had not discovered freely falling folds. The Greek music drama in relation to the entire art of antiquity is like that free arrangement of the folds: everything unfree, everything isolated in the individual art forms, is overcome: at their communal sacrificial festivals hymns are sung to beauty *and* at the same time to audacity. Tightly bound and yet possessing grace, a diversity and simultaneously a unity, many arts working at their highest level and yet one *single* artwork — that is the ancient music drama. Whoever looks at it and is reminded of the ideal espoused by a certain contemporary reformer of art will, at the same time, say to himself that this artwork of the future[28] is by no means a gleaming, yet deceptive, mirage: what we hope for the future is something that was once reality — in a past of more than two thousand years.

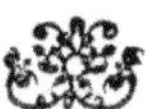

Endnoten

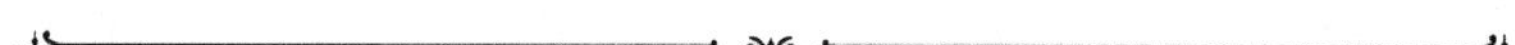

1.

"Das griechische Musikdrama," *Gesammelte Werke* [Musarion-Ausgabe] ed. Richard Oehler, Max Oehler, and Friedrich Chr. Wurzbach, 33 vols (Munich: Musarion, 1920–1929) vol. 3, *Die Geburt der Tragödie; Aus dem Gedankenkreis der Geburt der Tragödie, 1869–1871*, 169–87. Our text is an exact replication of the Musarion edition of the GMD, save in two ways: 0) we have included paragraph breaks whenever Nietzsche uses a lengthy quote; and 1) we have adopted the corrections to the text made by Paolo D'Iorio & noted on the website Nietzsche Source. Finally, any differences between editions have been observed in the notes herein. GMD can also be found in *Werke* [Großoktavausgabe] ed. F. Koegel, 19 vols (Leipzig: Neumann, 1895–1897; 2 edn, 1899–1913) vol. 9, 33–52.

2.

The Musarion and the *Großoktavausgabe* editions omit the following passage, which can be found in the KGW and KSA: "in den fortwährenden Widersprüchen der angeblichen Überlieferung und des natürlichen Gehör's kam man dahin, Musik gar nicht mehr für das Ohr, sondern für das Auge zu componieren. Die Augen sollten das contrapunktische Geschick des Componisten bewundern: die Augen sollten die Ausdrucksfähigkeit der Musik anerkennen. Wie war dies zu bewerkstelligen? Man färbte die Noten mit der Farbe der Dinge, von denen im Texte die Rede war, also grün, wenn Pflanzen, Felder Weinberge, purpurroth, wenn die Sonne und das Licht erwähnt wurden." KSA 1, 517.

3.

The KGW and the KSA have "Masse" and not "Menge."

Endnotes

1.

Nietzsche's identification of the Locrian mode with the Dorian mode glosses over the distinction between mode and scale, and the differences between medieval and modern terminology. The main source for ancient Greek music theory is Aristoxenus of Tarentum, of whose writings (from the third century BCE) on harmonics and on rhythm various incomplete books survive, while later sources include Boethius' *De institutione musica* (from the sixth century CE), Hucbald's *De harmonica institutione* (from the ninth century CE), and the anonymous treatise *Alia musica*. For further discussion of the Dorian mode, cf. one of Nietzsche's sources (see below), August Wilhelm Ambros' *Geschichte der Musik*, vol. 1, 380-404; as well as Phillips Barry, "Greek Music," *The Musical Quarterly* 5 (1919) 578-613, and the entries on "Mode" and "Scale" in *The New Grove Dictionary of Music*. Strictly speaking, the Locrian mode corresponds to the Hyperdorian mode, but Nietzsche's reference to the Dorian mode is strategic, in that the Greeks believed in a link between music and character (Plato, *Republic*, 401 and 402; *Laws*, 659c–659e; Aristotle, *Politics*, 1340b). In the *Laches*, Socrates' eponymous interlocutor remarks that "the true musician" is "attuned to a fairer harmony than that of the lyre, or any pleasant instrument of music, for truly he has in his own life a harmony of words and deeds arranged — not in the Ionian, or in the Phrygian mode, nor yet in the Lydian, but in the true Hellenic mode, which is the Dorian, and no other" (188d), and Socrates concurs that "the Dorian mode [...] is a harmony of words and deeds" (193e). In the *Republic*, Socrates counsels avoidance of the Lydian, Mixolydian, and Ionian modes, but implicitly recommends Dorian or Phrygian modes for soldiers (398d–399c; Plato, *The Collected Dialogues*, eds Edith Hamilton and Huntington Cairns (Princeton, N.J.: Princeton University Press, 1963) 132, 137, 643–44), while Aristotle in his *Politics* (1340b) describes the effect of the Dorian as being able to produce "a moderate and settled temper." See Aristotle, *Basic Works*, ed. Richard McKeon (New York: Random House, 1941)

1312. In Nietzsche's own time, Gilbert, in Oscar Wilde's dialogue "The Critic as Artist" (1891), says of the overture to Wagner's *Tannhäuser*: "To-morrow, like the music of which Aristotle and Plato tell us, the noble Dorian music of the Greek, it may perform the office of a physician, and give us an anodyne against pain, and heal the spirit that is wounded, & 'bring the soul into harmony with all right things.'" This perhaps is an allusion to Plato's *Republic* (401d): "Rhythm and harmony find their way to the inmost soul and take strongest hold upon it, bringing with them and imparting grace." See *Collected Dialogues*, 646. Wilde's character concludes: "What is true of music is true about all the arts. Beauty has as many meanings as man has moods. Beauty is the symbol of symbols. Beauty reveals everything, because it expresses nothing. When it shows itself, it shows us the whole fiery-colored world." Oscar Wilde, *Plays, Prose Writings, and Poems* (London: Dent; New York: Dutton, 1930) 1–65 [see 28]. Elsewhere, in *The Birth of Tragedy* (§2 and §4), Nietzsche uses the term Doric with reference to one of the four major tribes of ancient Greece, singling out Doric art as immortalizing "the majestic and rejecting attitude of Apollo" (KSA 1, 32), describing the music of Apollo as "Doric architectonic in tones" (KSA 1, 33), and calling the Doric state a "military encampment" of the Apollonian (KSA 1, 41). In 1888, Nietzsche returns to the problem of drama and the Doric: "The word *drama* is of Doric origin: and according to Doric usage it means 'event,' 'story,' both words in a hieratic sense. The most ancient drama represented the legend of a place, or the 'holy story' on which the foundation of a cult rested (— in other words, not something that is done, but something that happens: *drām* in Doric doesn't mean 'to do')." This is stated in a footnote in *The Case of Wagner* §9; KSA 6, 32; cf. KSA 13, 145[34], 235. A better understanding of the thinking and implications behind Nietzsche's equation of the Dorian and the Locrian remains a desideratum for further research, beyond the scope of this translation.

2.

See Voltaire's poem of 1751, addressed to Angelo Maria Quirini (1860–1755), an Italian cardinal and a member of the Academies of Science of Berlin, Vienna, and Russia. See Voltaire, *Épître* 81, "À Monsieur le Cardinal Quirini," *Œuvres complètes de Voltaire*, ed. Louis Moland, 52 vols (Paris: Garnier, 1877–1885) vol. 10, 357–58.

3.

Of the various periods of ancient Greek comedy, New Comedy, following the periods of Old Comedy and Middle Comedy, is associated with the writings of Menander, and Latin adaptations by Plautus and Terence.

4.

This constitutes Nietzsche's first use of the term *genealogisch*; in his later works, he will argue that the meaning of an object can be revealed by tracing its origin, which is uncovered by genealogy.

5.

Aeschylus (c. 525 to c. 455–456 BCE) was considered by many (including A.W. Schlegel, in his *Lectures on Dramatic Art and Literature*, lecture 6) to be the creator of tragedy, and Sophocles (c. 497–496 to c. 406–405 BCE) one of its greatest exponents. For a recent discussion of the significance of tragedy in general, see Charles Freeman, *The Greek Achievement: The Foundation of the Western World* (New York: Viking, 1999).

6.

The *Musarion* and the *Großoktavausgabe* editions omit the following passage, which can be found in the KGW and KSA: "In the continuous contradictions between what had supposedly been handed down and one's natural sense of pitch one ended up no longer writing music for the ears, but for the eyes. The eyes were supposed to admire the contrapuntal dexterity of the composer.

How was this to be brought about? The notes were colored with the color of things that were mentioned in the text; hence green, when plants, fields, vineyards, or crimson, when the sun and the light were mentioned." KSA 1, 517.

7.

Nietzsche will use similar coinages later, in *Thus Spoke Zarathustra* for instance, when in "On Redemption" he speaks of "human beings who are nothing more than a large eye, or a large mouth or a large belly or anything at all large — inverse cripples I call such beings." Z: II.20; KSA 4, 182.

8.

Anselm Feuerbach (1829–1880) was a German classicist painter, the son of the archaeologist and philologist Joseph Anselm Feuerbach (1798–1851) & the grandson of Paul Johann Anselm Ritter von Feuerbach (1775–1833), among whose other sons was the philosopher Ludwig Feuerbach (1804–1872).

9.

The figure of the "messenger" (*angelos* or *exangelos*) is exemplified in *Oedipus the King* by the first messenger, who announces the choice of Oedipus as their king by the people of Isthmus, and the second messenger, who narrates the death of Jocasta. For further discussion, see James Barrett, *Staged Narrative: Poetics and the Messenger in Greek Tragedy* (Berkeley, CA, and London: University of California Press, 2002).

10.

Anselm Feuerbach, *Der vatikanische Apollo: Eine Reihe archäologisch-ästhetischer Betrachtungen* [1833] 2nd edn (Stuttgart and Augsburg: Cotta, 1855) 282–83. Translated by PB. According to Giorgio Colli's & Mazzino Montinari's commentary, Nietzsche borrowed this book from the University Library in Basel on 26 November 1869 (KSA 14, 99).

11.

Here Nietzsche uses the verb *aneignen*, in much the same way that Goethe, in *Faust I*, writes: "What we are born with, we must make our own / Or it remains a mere appurtenance / And is not ours" (*Was du ererbt von deinen Vätern hast, / Erwirb es, um es zu besitzen*) ll. 684–85; Goethe, *Faust: Part One*, tr. David Luke (Oxford and New York: Oxford University Press, 1987) 25. These lines were one of Freud's favorite quotations from Goethe.

12.

Lessing, *Hamburgische Dramaturgie*, vol. 1, no. 2: "There was only *one* Athens, and there will only ever be *one* Athens, where even in the masses the ethical feeling was so fine, so delicate, that actors and authors of a dubious morality ran the risk of being hounded from the theater!" Lessing, *Werke in fünf Bänden*, ed. Karl Balser, 5 vols (Berlin and Weimar: Aufbau-Verlag, 1982) vol. 4, 19. Translated by PB.

13.

Compare with *The Birth of Tragedy* §1: "In the German Middle Ages, too, singing and dancing crowds, ever increasing in number, whirled themselves from place to place under this same Dionysian impulse. In these dancers of St. John & St. Vitus, we rediscover the Bacchic choruses of the Greeks, with their prehistory in Asia Minor, as far back as Babylon and the orgiastic Sacaea." *Basic Writings of Nietzsche*, ed. and tr. Walter Kaufmann (New York: Modern Library, 1968) 36 (KSA 1, 29); cf. KSA 7, 1[1], 10; 1[33]–[34], 19; 7[50], 150; *Human, All Too Human*, vol. 1, §214 (KSA 2, 174); cf. KSA 8, 23[11], 406.

14.

In the German translation of Shakespeare's *A Midsummer Night's Dream*, set in Athens and a nearby wood, the figure of Bottom is called Zettel, the name used here by Nietzsche. The commentary

in KGW III.5/2, 1469, draws attention to the following passage in Richard Wagner's essay on "Beethoven," also published in 1870: "Whoever allows himself to be influenced by the views I have here expressed in regard of Beethovenian music, will certainly not escape being called fantastic and extravagant; and this reproach will be leveled at him not merely by our educated and uneducated musicians of the day — who for the most part have seen that dream-vision of Music's under no other guise than Bottom's dream in the *Midsummer's Night* — but in particular by our literary poets and even our plastic artists, so far as they ever trouble their heads with questions that seem to lie entirely beyond their sphere." Richard Wagner, *Actors and Singers*, tr. William Ashton Ellis (Lincoln, NB & London: University of Nebraska Press, 1995) 57–126 [see 113]; cf. *Sämtliche Schriften und Dichtungen* [*Volks-Ausgabe*] 16 in 8 vols (Leipzig: Breitkopf & Härtel/Siegel, 1911) vol. 9, 61–126 [see 112].

15.

Compare with Nietzsche's remarks on the lyric poet in *The Birth of Tragedy* §5: "The lyric genius is conscious of a world of images and symbols — growing out of his state of mystical self-abnegation and oneness. [...] The images of the *lyrist* are nothing but *his very* self and, as it were, only different projections of himself [...]." *Basic Writings of Nietzsche*, 50; KSA 1, 44–45.

16.

In their commentary (KSA 14, 99), Colli and Montinari suggest an allusion to the *Phaedo*, 69c, where Socrates says: "You know how the initiation practitioners say, 'Many bear the emblems, but the devotees are few?'" Plato, *Collected Dialogues*, 52.

17.

See Gottfried Semper, *Der Stil in den technischen und tektonischen Künsten, oder, Praktische Aesthetik: Ein Handbuch für Techniker, Künstler und Kunstfreunde*, 2 vols (Frankfurt am Main:

Verlag für Kunst und Wissenschaft, 1860–1863) vol. 1, *Die textile Kunst für sich betrachtet und in Beziehung zur Baukunst*, 75. Tr. by PB.

18.

See Aristotle's definition of tragedy in his *Poetics* §6, which includes the following: "Every tragedy has six constituents, which will determine its quality. These are plot, character, diction, thought, spectacle, and song." *Classical Literary Criticism*, 39.

19.

See A.W. Schlegel, *Vorlesungen über dramatische Kunst und Literatur*, Lecture 5, in *Kritische Schriften und Briefe*, ed. Edgar Lohner (Stuttgart: Kohlhammer, 1962–1974) vol. 5, 61–71 (esp. 64–66). See also *The Birth of Tragedy* §7: "A.W. Schlegel [...] advises us to regard the chorus somehow as the essence and extract of the crowd of spectators — as the 'ideal spectator.' This view, when compared with the historical tradition that originally tragedy was only chorus, reveals itself for what it is — a crude, unscientific, yet brilliant claim that owes its brilliancy only to its concentrated form of expression, to the typically Germanic bias in favor of anything called 'ideal,' and to our momentary astonishment." *Basic Writings of Nietzsche*, 56–57; KSA 1, 53.

20.

"Speaking trumpet," if quaint to the 21st-century ear, is the closest equivalent to the word Nietzsche uses in German, and the actual device the word refers to; it is then a *technologically* suitable translation. Both Sir Samuel Morland and Athanasius Kircher claim to have invented the device, and their partisans hotly contest who actually deserves credit for inventing it. The modern equivalent of it is "megaphone," but that word was not coined until 1878, possibly by Edison, hence almost ten years after Nietzsche wrote GMD. In German, megaphone is very specifically "*Megafon*" or "*Sprachrohr*."

On the claims of Morland and Kircher, see *The Penny Cyclopædia of the Society for the Diffusion of Useful Knowledge*: Signio—Steam-Vessel (London: Charles Knight and Co., 1842) vol. 22, 322.

21.

See *Ars poetica*, 189 (*Classical Literary Criticism*, 85): "If you want your play to be called for and given a second performance, it should not be either shorter or longer than five acts."

22.

See Mozart's opera *Don Giovanni*, Act 2.

23.

August Wilhelm Ambros, *Geschichte der Musik*, 5 vols (Leipzig: Leuckart, 1862–1868) vol. 1, 288; tr. by PB. On the west pediment of the Parthenon temple in Athens, the goddess of wisdom and war, Athena, and the sea-god Poseidon, were depicted in competition for the patronage of the city. For further discussion of this image, see Ernest Arthur Gardner, "Athene in the West Pediment of the Parthenon," *The Journal of Hellenic Studies* 3 (1882) 244–255.

24.

The preface to the published version (1769) of the opera *Alceste* (first performed 1767), based on the tragedy *Alceste* by Euripides, sets out the principles for the reform of opera elaborated by Christoph Willibald Gluck (1714–1787); notably, greater prominence should be given to the chorus.

25.

Compare with Schopenhauer's idea in *The World as Will and Representation*, vol. 1 §52, that, in music, the will-to-life itself becomes in some sense visible: "Music is as *immediate* an objectification and copy of the whole *will* as the world itself is [...]. Therefore music is by no means like the other arts, namely a copy of the Ideas, but

a copy of the will itself." Schopenhauer, *The World as Will and Representation*, tr. E.F.J. Payne, 2 vols (New York: Dover, 1969) vol. 1, 257.

26.

See "Socrates and Tragedy," KSA 1, 533–49.

27.

Ambros, *Geschichte der Musik*, vol. 1, 290.

28.

An obvious reference to Richard Wagner and his treatise, *The Artwork of the Future* (*Das Kunstwerk der Zukunft*) (1849). According to the entry in Cosima Wagner's diary for 11 June 1870, Nietzsche read his lecture to Wagner and Rohde during a visit to Triebschen, but Wagner disapproved of the title. See Dieter Borchmeyer and Jörg Salaquarda (eds), *Nietzsche und Wagner: Stationen einer epochalen Begegnung*, 2 vols (Frankfurt am Main: Insel, 1994) vol. 2, 1158. For the possible cause of Wagner's discontent, see Cosima's response in her letter to Nietzsche of 24 June 1870, cited above (*Nietzsche und Wagner*, vol. 1, 89–90).

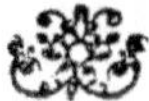

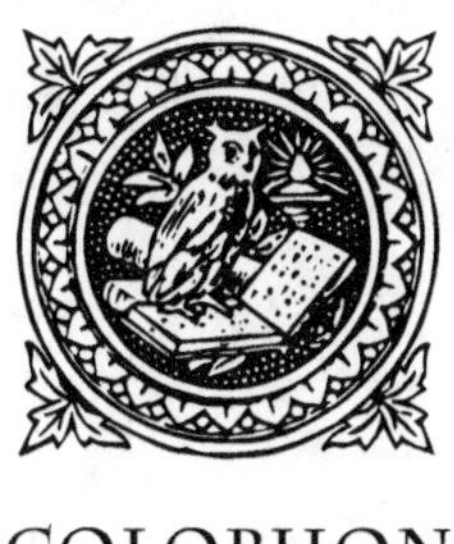

COLOPHON

THE GREEK MUSIC DRAMA was typeset in InDesign 5.0.
The text, titles, and page numbers are set in *Adobe Jenson Pro.*

Book design & typesetting: Alessandro Segalini
Cover design: Alessandro Segalini

THE GREEK MUSIC DRAMA

is published by Contra Mundum Press
and printed by Lightning Source, which has received Chain of
Custody certification from: The Forest Stewardship Council,
The Programme for the Endorsement of Forest Certification,
and The Sustainable Forestry Initiative.

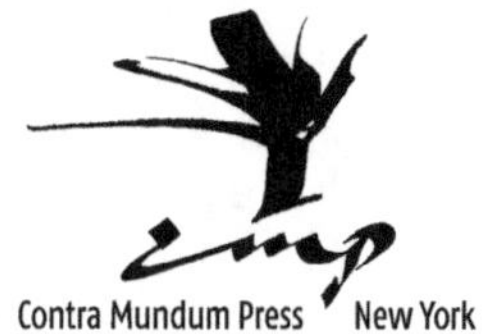

CONTRA MUNDUM PRESS

Contra Mundum Press is dedicated to the value & the indispensable importance of the individual voice.

Contra Mundum Press will be publishing titles from all the fields in which the genius of the age traditionally produces the most challenging and innovative work: poetry, novels, theatre, philosophy — including philosophy of science & of mathematics — criticism, and essays. Upcoming volumes include Richard Foreman's *Plays with Films*, Louis Auguste Blanqui's *Eternity by the Stars*, & Fernando Pessoa's *Transformation Book*.

For the complete list of forthcoming publications, please visit our website. To be added to our mailing list, send your name and email address to: info@contramundum.net

Contra Mundum Press
P.O. Box 1326
New York, NY 10276
USA
http://contramundum.net

OTHER CONTRA MUNDUM PRESS TITLES

Gilgamesh
Ghérasim Luca, *Self-Shadowing Prey*
Rainer J. Hanshe, *The Abdication*
Walter Jackson Bate, *Negative Capability*
Miklós Szentkuthy, *Marginalia on Casanova*
Fernando Pessoa, *Philosophical Essays*
Elio Petri, *Writings on Cinema & Life*
Friedrich Nietzsche, *The Greek Music Drama*

SOME FORTHCOMING TITLES

Richard Foreman, *Plays with Films*
Miklós Szentkuthy, *Towards the One & Only Metaphor*
William Wordsworth, *The Sublime & the Beautiful*
Louis Auguste Blanqui, *Eternity by the Stars*
Emilio Villa, *The Selected Poems of Emilio Villa*
Robert Kelly, *A Voice Full of Cities: Collected Essays*
Jean-Jacques Rousseau, *Narcissus*
Fernando Pessoa, *The Transformation Book*

www.ingramcontent.com/pod-product-compliance
Lightning Source LLC
LaVergne TN
LVHW061224100826
845148LV00004B/856

* 9 7 8 0 9 8 3 6 9 7 2 7 5 *